MW00791762

Doing Business
with Singapore

Paul Leppert

JAIN PUBLISHING COMPANY
Fremont, California

This book is designed to provide helpful information for people doing business with Singapore. It is sold with the understanding that it is not meant to render legal, medical, accounting, or other professional advice. For such services contact a competent practitioner. Some are listed in this book.

Library of Congress Cataloging-in-Publication Data

Leppert, Paul A.
    [Doing business in Singapore]
    Doing business with Singapore / Paul Leppert.
       p.   cm. — (Global business series)
    Originally published: Doing business in Singapore. Chula Vista, Calif.: Patton Pacific Press, c1990, in series: Asian business series.
    Includes index.
    ISBN 0-87573-042-6
    1. Singapore—Economic conditions. 2. Singapore—Social conditions. 3. United States—Foreign economic relations—Singapore. 4. Singapore—Foreign economic relations—United States. 5. Business etiquette—Singapore. I. Title.
II. Series.
HC445.8.L47   1995
658.8'48'095957—dc20   95-14751
                                       CIP

Contents

Introduction

The Pacific Rim is the world's biggest business arena. It contains sixty per cent of the world's population and a three trillion dollar a year economy which is growing about three billion dollars per week. The United States trades more with Pacific Rim nations than with the rest of the world combined.

In recent years the ability of the United States to export to the Pacific Rim has been so weak that ships steaming from the United States to Asia have departed with many empty holds. The same ships return to the United States fully loaded with Asian products. At times shipping rates to Asia have been half the rates from Asia.

The United States seems able to sell goods to Asia only by offering fire sale prices. Since the end of World War II the dollar has lost more than three-quarters its value in Japanese Yen.

The *Global Business Series* is designed to help American business succeed globally. This book addresses opportunities and problems in doing business with Singapore.

The first part of this book covers the cultural and social environment which affects business in Singapore. Culture is the prime determinant of human conduct. It must be understood to do business effectively. One cannot do business with a cultural stereotype.

The second part deals with the economic and business environment in Singapore. It explains how the economy originated and developed, its successes, problems, opportunities, and pitfalls. Of particular importance are Singapore's business procedures, bargaining techniques, and ways to get business help.

The final section is concerned with your personal experience of Singapore: travel tips; things to do, see, and learn; living conditions, useful addresses, and recommended reading.

This book is based largely on material gathered from interviews with business people in Singapore. It is designed as a guide to start you in this market. It is not intended to offer advice for specific business situations. Conditions in Singapore are constantly changing. Organizations listed in this book may be contacted for the most recent information. This book does not represent the positions of any agencies of the governments of the United States or Singapore.

Prices are denominated in United States dollars unless otherwise specified.

PART ONE

Knowing Your Counterpart

Asians have different business goals and procedures from ours because their cultures hold different values. To understand these people we need to know how they view themselves, their families, society, work, culture, and politics. The answers are complicated because Singapore has many diverse cultures: Malay, Chinese, Indian, and Western. All must be understood to do business effectively.

When two people from different cultures do business, each acts and reacts according to cultural patterns established in childhood. These indelible imprints like the delicately etched circuits of computer chips program both social and business behavior. If you understand your counterpart's cultural conditioning, you will go into a business situation with a decided advantage. To a certain extent you will be able to predict his or her behavior. You can be sure your counterpart will be studying *your* cultural conditioning.

Understanding another culture with its vast, deep, complicated currents is not easy. In addition to obtaining a business advantage you will receive, as a bonus, a new understanding of your own culture. Your perspective on life will never be quite the same.

1. *Knowing Your Counterpart: Culture and Society*

Settlement of Southeast Asia

How did the tiny island of Singapore, a speck in the seas of Southeast Asia, achieve such importance in world business? The answers may be found in the surrounding land and its people.

Viewed from the plane the bright glare of the tropical rain forest conceals a dark secret. The high lush canopy of treetops consumes all the life-giving sunlight. Beneath the dense glitter of green foliage it is perpetual night, a rotting dank hollow with little life.

In scattered places there is some farming. Slash and burn clearing of the forest for a single quick crop rapidly depletes soils already leached by torrential rains.

It would be hard to find a more hostile environment. One wonders: who first came here and why?

The answers begin far to the northwest in the high Himalayas. Here rocky summits spawn sharp ridges which fall to the southeast, flaying apart like fingers to form the rugged islands and peninsulas of Southeast Asia. In the watersheds between these ridges flow some of Asia's great rivers, the Irrawaddy, Sittang, Salween, Chao Phraya, Mekong, and the Red. Early immigrants followed the flowing water from mountain to sea. Others, part of a sailing society which stretched from the east coast of Africa to Easter Island in the eastern Pacific, arrived in boats. These maritime people, the first Malays, lived by fishing, trade, and piracy.

3

In time the area came under the influence of Indian culture. Centuries later a prince of the Indo-Malay kingdom of Sri Vijaya founded a city on an island off the Malay Peninsula. He named it after animals he had seen in the area: Singapore, City of the Lions.

The Emerald Island

Singapore's very name stirs memories of a romantic past. Like a glistening jewel at an estate sale it evokes a bygone era, an age of Raffles and Singapore slings, of sultans and sundry Malay kings, whist on white verandas under a sultry sun. Singapore recalls the great age of Britain's Victorian empire, cream and alabaster manors, the staid old Cricket Club, and the Raffles Hotel where Kipling, Maugham, and Conrad penned immortal classics.

It was an age of power and glory. But it was based on sound business decisions. Singapore was founded to promote commerce. It was born to do business. And it succeeded. The island city was a jewel in the crown of Britain's Asian empire for over a hundred years and remains a world business center today.

During the Victorian era everyday life for British colonists on the Emerald Island centered on commerce. Life near the equator was relaxed if not languid. The weather and hours of daylight were much the same the year around. Nature provided no schedules so civilized gentlemen invented their own. On special occasions pomp and parade proved the power of British starch in the face of the withering local humidity.

But daily life was less ostentatious. A British colonist of the period arose early to enjoy a walk or horseback ride while the morning was still cool. Returning home he changed into pajamas for a snack of coffee, biscuit, and fruit while reading on the veranda. For a dollar a month a Hindu barber came by to provide a shave. Breakfast of fish, curry, eggs, rice, and claret began at nine.

Office hours started at ten. Work involved accounting, finance, purchasing, and marketing. In the world before computers, the pace was slower, a casual commerce. There was a break for tiffin at one. This usually consisted of curried rice, fruit, and more claret. Work resumed at two and lasted until four-thirty. Immediately after work there was often a game of cricket or a band concert on the esplanade. By six our colonist was back home enjoying refreshment of sherry and bitters.

Dinner at seven on teak tables was a tableau of gleaming white jackets, gauze gowns, and waving punkahs under argon lamps, a feast of fish and fowl, mounds of mutton, sliced turkey, curried capons, spiced cabbage, imported cheeses, mangoes, rambutans, pomelos, plantains, and pineapples. Conversation centered on news brought by the latest ship.

The ladies soon disappeared in swishes of silk taffeta. For the men, cigars, more sherry, and the dinner was over. There was an hour or two for billiards and books. Then it was time to retire. Not a bad life.

In contrast the area's Malays, Chinese, and Indians often lived in base poverty. In nearby Malaya they toiled long hours in dank tin mines and on sweltering rubber plantations for meager wages. On the island Asians were employed as laborers and servants. Few of their grandchildren have wistful yearnings for the imperial past.

Today, Singapore is a modern multiracial state. Seventy-seven per cent of the population is Chinese, fifteen per cent is Malay, six per cent Indian or Pakistani, and two per cent Eurasian or European. Singapore has four official languages: Malay, Chinese (Mandarin), Tamil, and English. The national language is Malay. English is the primary language of business.

Singapore's appearance is so modern that it is easy to forget that its heart is Asian. The Indian restaurant owner still wears a wraparound skirt and eats food off a banana leaf. But he uses closed-circuit television to find you an empty seat and adds your bill on a calculator. The Chinese electronics executive may end your meeting early so he can visit a Taoist temple to find a geomancer to locate his new house in a way which will not disturb the spirits. Indeed, the doors of the new Hyatt Hotel were sited by a Chinese geomancer.

Many common superstitions concern pregnancy. If a pregnant woman breaks crab legs her baby will have problems walking. Unripe fruit causes miscarriages. Eating soy sauce causes a dark-skinned baby. Digesting mangoes causes a newborn's skin to blotch. A diet of green vegetables causes excessive bleeding at childbirth. Eating mutton produces a stupid baby with sheep's eyes.

THE MALAYS

Religions

The earliest Malays were animists. Both Hinduism and Buddhism exerted early influences. In time these were largely replaced by Islam. Islam first arrived in Southeast Asia with Moslem merchants from India who refused to do business with infidels. The Malays, an easygoing people, were quickly converted. By the time Marco Polo passed through the area in 1292 the Malays were mostly Moslem.

Islam was founded by the Prophet Muhammad in the seventh century. It replaced ancient polytheistic religions with a belief in one God. Muhammad established his first Islamic community in the city of Medina after a flight from Mecca. In 632 Muhammad led a pilgrimage *(baj)* from Medina back to Mecca. Today many Moslems repeat this visit as a religious obligation.

Islam unified the warring tribes of Arabs and soon spread to large areas of the Middle East, Africa, and Asia. The Koran, the holy book of Islam, defines a religion which enters every aspect of the lives of its adherents through a strict code called *Sharia*.

Islam has its version of filial piety. The *Hadith,* sayings of the prophet, states that one will not even get a whiff of the fragrance of heaven unless one shows respect for one's parents.

Islam absorbed many older Malay beliefs but in the process was itself changed. Mosques were built on the sites of Buddhist and Hindu temples. The spirits of Malay folk religion were given the names of Islamic angels and devils. The sacred fowl of the Hindu god Vishnu was recast as the Garuda, the big bird in *The Tale of The Arabian Nights.*

The Islamic veneer which covers Malay animism is indeed very thin. Many Malays observe the one month daylight fast of Ramadan only on the last day. Few eat pork but many partake of alcohol, which is also forbidden by Islam.

In Malay animism, every entity of nature, including rocks, trees, and animals, has a spirit which is part of *semangat,* the vital force of nature which permeates and animates all things. These spirits possess great powers of good and evil. Only the *pawang,* the shaman, is capable of appeasing them. Even seasoned lumber is deemed to possess a tree-soul which must be propitiated by an invocation performed when launching ships.

Malays, like many Southeast Asians, scan the skies for signs, listen to the stars and planets, consult sorcerers, trust fortune tellers, and beg the spirits for fertile fields and strong sons. They view *semangat* as the generic inspiration for all religions.

Language

Malay is a member of the Indonesian language family. Malay and Indonesian were once the same language. But by the nineteenth century Malay was heavily influenced by English and Indonesian was influenced by Dutch. Today they are best described as mutually intelligible dialects. Officially Bahasa Malay is the language of both nations.

Written Malay is spelled phonetically. The grammar is simple. Plurals are usually expressed by repeating the noun.

Anak is child. The term for children is *anak anak*. It is written as *anak 2*.

There are no tense changes in Malay. One just adds *suda* to make anything past tense. In spoken practice articles such as a, or an, are omitted. So is the verb to be. Vowels are short. The accent is always on the last syllable. Like all languages Malay reflects ethnocentric biases. Orangutans are called *orang utan*. Aborigines, such as the Negritos, are called *orang asli*.

Stamford Raffles, the founder of Singapore, set a good example for all business people by mastering Malay on the boat trip from Britain.

Music and Dance

Malay music often involves drama, dance, and religious ritual. Much of it originated in nearby Indonesia and was brought to Singapore by laborers from Java. There are also Arab and Portuguese influences.

Instruments include a variety of rattan braced wooden drums; tambourines, such as the *tar* and *kompang;*, flutes; gongs, such as the *canang* and *rnung;* the *tali*, a three-stringed spiked fiddle; and the *kertok*, a single bar xylophone using a large coconut as a resonator.

The best known Malay music is performed by *gamelan* (gong and chime) ensembles. This type of music was first developed on the Indonesian island of Java and uses bronze drums tuned to three, four, and six notes.

The *wayang kulit*, a shadow-puppet theater, is a form of drama which originated in nearby Indonesia. The puppeteer, to the accompaniment of music, dramatizes stories from the *Ramayana*.

The monkey dance, which I viewed one night long ago in a fire-lit temple on the island of Bali, is a stone-age ritual in which the dancers and the audience become possessed by the spirits of animals. It resurrects a primordial past in which primitive not-yet-human beings could speak with animals. In the seductive tinkle of the tambourines, the enchanting beat of the *gendang* drum, and the trance inducing low of the *tali* one's soul is captured and carried far beyond the flickering shadows on the temple wall to a blessed past inhabited by protean beasts, a hallowed world before our species.

Art and Architecture

The arts of Singapore and the surrounding area consist of a multi-cultured mosaic of Indonesian, Hindu, Buddhist, Islamic, and Chinese tiles which are held in place by Malay grout.

Malay art arose from the innate talent of Malays for craftsmanship. It was a natural evolution from the practical to the sublime. Early Malay art involved the decoration of useful objects such as clothes, boats, and houses. Since these things were soon destroyed by heat and humidity, Malays had little interest in creating art "for eternity." Little remains of their wood and fiber art. Only objects of stone, pottery, brick, and bronze have survived. Today they may be seen in the national museum.

The art of creating *batik* was first developed in Java by Malay people in the Twelfth Century. Hot wax is applied to parts of a pattern drawn from cotton or silk. The cloth is dipped in indigo for two days. Wax is added and removed from different parts of the pattern between each dyeing. By hand the process takes months. It is imitated in minutes by machines in Singapore.

Early Malay artisans were available on a mass scale to create the temples of central Java. The inspiration for these monuments did not come from Malay culture but originated in Hindu and Buddhist concepts from India. These structures, with their human statuary, celebrate a concept of life which makes no distinction between the holy and the worldly. Both are seen as one with the cosmos.

Bronze-age technology from southern China enabled Malays to develop the metal kettle drums used for music and dance.

Festivals and Holidays

If you like festivals, you will like Singapore, for it has many. Moslems, Hindus, and Chinese follow the lunar calendar, so the same festival will fall on different days of the Western calendar in different years.

Most Moslem holidays are associated with the holy month of Ramadan. Fifteen days before the start of Ramadan the souls of the dead visit the homes of their families on Nisfu Night.

The arrival of the Koran on earth is celebrated during Ramadan on the Night of Grandeur. *Isra Dan Mi' Raj,* which falls between June and September, celebrates the prophet's ascension.

THE INDIANS

Origins

Indian contact with the area around Singapore began about the first century, A.D. when traders from the Coromandel Coast of South India began to visit the area. The number of Indian residents was quite small until the nineteenth century when the rubber plantations on the Malay Peninsula expanded in response to the demand for tires by the emerging vehicle industry in the United States and Europe. Most of the planters came from India and brought Indian labor. Today about two-thirds of the Indians in Singapore are Tamil descendants of this work force. The rest are mostly from Kerala.

Philosophy and Religion

Early Indian traders introduced Hindu and Buddhist ideas and culture. These religions developed side-by-side and supplemented rather than replaced Malay animism.

Some Indians in Singapore are Moslems, but most are Hindu. Hinduism is often viewed as a religion with many gods, sub-gods, saints, lords, and holy men. Some experts do not consider Hinduism polytheistic because it subscribes to one Universal Spirit called Brahma (world soul) which has a trinity of forms: Brahma, the Creator; Vishnu, the Preserver; and Shiva, the Destroyer.

Hindus believe that all living things have souls which wander after physical death. In time the souls bind to higher or lower forms of life, depending upon how the former owner of the soul behaved. To have a good transmigration, one had to observe strictly the religious obligations prescribed by the Brahmans (Hindu priests). The Brahmans created and maintained a social system in which darker people had lower cast. Each caste had strict rules for employment and conduct. One caste was "untouchable" and did the dirty work.

Hinduism was once the dominate religion of Malaya and Indonesia. Today it is a majority religion only on the island of Bali. But many of Singapore's Indians are Hindus.

Buddhism also came from India. It was founded by Siddhartha Gautama, the Buddha, who was born in 503 B.C. He rebelled against the Hindu hagiarchy by asserting that the transmigration of souls was caused by craving for wealth and power. These sad wanderings of spirits could be ended only by eliminating such lusts. Only then could a soul achieve Nirvana, the "blowing out" of the flame called the soul. Gautama's Eight-fold Path to Nirvana includes right belief, elimination of sensual pleasure and cruelty, moderation in all things, and meditation. Although Buddhism began as a protest against Hinduism, the two religions have existed together for many years.

Music and Dance

Indian music is often related to festivals. On such days music recorded from the soundtracks of Tamil films may be played in temples. Sometimes small ensembles perform.

In Indian music the drums are much more dominant than in Malay or Chinese music. Drummers can offer more sophisticated renditions because they are not required to keep the beat. In Indian music the cymbals, clappers, and gongs keep the time.

There are hundreds of kinds of Indian folk instruments. Some achieved musical prominence in unusual ways. The *pungi,* a type of drone similar to a bagpipe, was first developed by snake charmers!

Serious Indian music follows a *sastra* or body of doctrine which Westerners might call canonical. Performers may play only in accordance with *raga* or melody patterns which are sharply defined.

Some Indian hymns are based on Tamil poems dating as far back as the seventh century. "The Garland of the Gods" sings praises to Shiva. The "Four Thousand Compositions" are devoted to Vishnu.

Festivals and Holidays

Most Indian festivals are of Hindu or Buddhist origin. The harvest festival, *Thai Pongal,* held on January 14th, celebrates the beginning of the Hindu month of *Thai,* the luckiest month of the year.

The festival of *Thaipusam* held in January or February celebrates Hinduism by exalting the community spirit. The mythical Lord Murugan (Subramaniam) is venerated on this sacred day. Worshipers petition this lord by bringing a *kavadi,* an offering carried on the shoulder, to his shrine. Hooks and spikes are passed from the *kavadi* through the worshiper's skin. They often pierce their tongues or cheeks with small silver spears. In Singapore *kavadi* are carried from Perumal Temple on Serangoon Road to Chettiar Temple on Tank Road. After the hooks and spikes are pulled from the skins of the *kavadi* bearers, holy ash is rubbed in the wounds. Thus purity of spirit is achieved.

In March or April in the full moon of the Tamil month of *Panguni* the *Panguni Uttiram,* festival for the marriages of Shiva to Shakti and Lord Subramanian to Theivani is celebrated. About the same time a nine-day festival is held by the Brahman caste to honor Sri Rama, the hero of the epic classic *Ramayana.*

In April or May *Chithirai Vishnu* celebrates the start of the Hindu New Year. During the same period Buddhists celebrate Vesak Day in which caged birds are released to symbolize the freeing of captive souls. The birth, Enlightenment, and passing of Buddha are celebrated on Vesak Day by offerings of flowers and fruit at local temples.

During July or August *Sri Krishna Jayanti,* a ten-day Hindu festival, celebrates events in Krishna's life. In August or September in the Hindu month of *Avani,* prayers are offered to the popular elephant-headed god called *Ganesh (Vinayagar).*

In September or October one may visit Sri Mariamnan Temple in Singapore to see the faithful test their faith by walking across beds of live coals. About the same time the Hindu festival of the Nine Nights is held at Chettiar Temple in dedication to the wives of Shiva, Vishnu, and Brahma.

Three important Hindu festivals fall between October and November. *Kantha Shashithi* honors Subramaniam and his fight against evil. *Deepavali* celebrates Rama's victory over a demon with the Festival of Lights involving thousands of small oil lamps. *Kartikai Deepani* recalls Shiva's transformation into a pillar of fire following an argument with Vishnu and Brahma.

On November 22nd Singapore's Sikhs celebrate the birthday of Guru Nanak who founded their religion in 1496.

THE CHINESE

Origins

Chinese traders visited Southeast Asia in ancient times. But there were only about one hundred fifty Chinese in

Singapore living on houseboats when Raffles rounded the
modern city in 1819. He encouraged the Chinese to immi-
grate and they arrived in droves. The opportunities in
Singapore looked good compared to the grinding poverty
and bureaucratic tyranny in their native land. Some came to
trade. But most arrived as indentured servants to work in tin
mines of nearby Malaya and as dock workers in the city. A
hardy and industrious people, the Chinese took jobs neither
the Indians nor the Malays would accept.

Today Chinese represent about three-quarters of the
population of Singapore. They are comprised of many lin-
guistic and provincial groups. Hokkien Chinese make up
about forty per cent of Singapore's population. Teochew Chinese represent twenty per cent. Most of the rest are of
Cantonese, Hainanese, and Hakka ancestry. Singapore today
is often called "the third China" after the Peoples Republic of
China and Taiwan.

Philosophy and Religion

Because of the Chinese numerical superiority, the ancient traditions of "the Middle Kingdom" provided much of
Singapore's cultural base. These are mostly Confucian traditions though there are many other influences. The great
teacher was born in 551 B.C. Confucius did not create his
ethical code but systematized one that already existed. His
social teachings were concerned with human relationships
and involved unequal obligations: the obedience of the son
to the father, of wife to husband, of younger brother to older
brother. Confucius stressed the virtues of thrift, harmony,
education, loyalty, and hard work. Many of these were similar
to the ideals of the Protestant Ethic which laid the foundation
for industrialization in the West. He never knew how much
his philosophy would facilitate the industrialization of East
Asia including Singapore.

Language

The government in Singapore is trying to encourage the use of Mandarin. A basic fluency in Mandarin is easier to obtain than most languages. There is little grammar so you need not spend time learning verb conjugations or noun declensions. The meaning is based on context, tonal inflections, and word order. If you plan to do business with Chinese in Singapore, it would be helpful to learn some Mandarin. Written Chinese is difficult to learn and requires the memorization of thousands of ideographic characters.

Music and Dance

Chinese immigrants to Singapore formed cultural societies to sustain their traditions. Here music and dance play an important part. Chinese music is as varied as the sounds of chants, gongs, and bells which fill the temples and the Western-style bands which play march music for funeral processions. Chinese opera is often performed in Singapore and extracts from Cantonese, Hokkien, and Teochew operas are regularly broadcast on the radio. A new type of popular music called "Mandarin Light" has been developed from the film scores of Chinese films.

Festivals and Holidays

The Chinese New Year begins on the first day of the lunar calendar in late January or early February. It marks a new beginning, a time to clean house, pay debts, visit relatives, have fun and feast. At this time you should give your employees and servants an extra month's pay in an *ang pow* (red envelope). The money should be in even amounts in new bills. Singapore has a strict policy for government ethics so *angpow* should not be given to public officials. Employees and servants are given four or five days off beginning with New Year's Eve.

Nine days after the New Year the Jade Festival honors the Chinese Ruler of Heaven. In March or April there are three important Chinese festivals: the birthday of Kuan Yin (the Goddess of Mercy), All Souls' Day (a time to visit family tombs), and the birthday of the Saint of the Poor (with a parade from White Cloud Temple on Ganges Avenue).

During April or May the birthday of Ma Cho Po, the Queen of Heaven and Goddess of the Sea is celebrated. In June the God of War, Kuan Ti has his birthday. Between June and August Singapore celebrates the Boat Festival. In China in ancient times at least one boat was capsized. The crew in drowning offered their lives to the god of fertility. Kuan Yin receives a second birthday party in July.

In August at the Festival of the Hungry Ghosts, a big party is held for the souls of the dead who are invited for a day of feasting and fun. After enjoying Chinese operas, these spirits eat only the essence of the banquets leaving the food itself to be consumed by their mortal hosts.

In September the Moon Festival celebrates the overthrow of the Mongol warlords in ancient China. Family groups gather to view the full moon and eat moon cakes. Between September and November Tua Pek Kong the God of Wealth is honored by Chinese Taoists who make a pilgrimage to his shrine on Kusu Island near Singapore.

In October or November Kuan Yin is honored with a third birthday! Chinese take no chances with this deity! Finally, in December the Winter Solstice or Harvest Festival is held.

Today most Chinese celebrate these festivals as holidays to be enjoyed rather than religious occasions.

THE NEW CULTURE

The West

The three Asian cultures of Singapore, Malay, Indian, and Chinese, have been influenced by a fourth. Western influence began with the arrival of Portuguese traders in the sixteenth century. By the time the British dominated the island, some three hundred years later, local Asians were feeling the full brunt of Western imperialism. Its aggressive mercantile spirit and confident Christianity left indelible marks such as the use of English for business and the colorful Easter and Christmas celebrations at Singapore's Church of St. Joseph.

Cultural Changes

From this great cultural diversity a common syncretic Singapore culture is emerging. Young and eclectic, it freely chooses the best from all traditions while rejecting the most rigid aspects of each. The island does not follow the Islamic custom of veiling women or the Indian caste systems. Such holidays as the month-long Market Festival and the August 9th celebration of Singapore's Independence are shared by all.

A basic question in Singapore's cultural development centers on whether modernization must mean Westernization. Western popular culture as found in television, comics, fast foods, and soft drinks has made significant inroads. Yet many Asian traditions remain strong. Perhaps Singapore will be one of the few nations to draw a reasonable balance between the stressful demands of modern business and the quiet spirits of its ancient cultures. The island's society is energetic, intelligent, prosperous, and self-confident, exactly the prerequisites for great cultural and economic achievements.

2. *Knowing Your Counterpart: Family Life*

Importance

Family life is particularly important to Asians. The socialization of children within the family creates powerful patterns which will remain with your counterpart for life. You will be dealing with the families of your customers, employees, bankers, and other business counterparts. Your understanding of the family system in Singapore will enhance your success.

Demographic Trends

Singapore was settled originally by male immigrants seeking work. Because they left their extended families behind most families in Singapore consist of only one or two generations. Despite this smaller size the typical Singapore family maintains a traditional Asian cohesion.

The integrity of the family is supported by the government. It takes an active role in family planning. The government rewards people who have no college education if they submit to sterilization after a first or second child. In contrast; parents with college degrees are given incentives to have many children. The government even sponsors "love boats" where educated single people can meet. These genetic manipulations are designed to improve the economy by producing a more competent work force.

Although education, housing, and medical care are subsidized by the government, Singapore is far from being a welfare state. As people gained confidence in the government's policies the growth in population slowed. People no longer feel they must have many children to support them in old age. Today the island no longer looks like a society composed of school aged children. From 1965 to 1980 the annual population increase fell from 3.5 per cent to 1.2 per cent. Demographers estimate Singapore will achieve zero population growth by 2020. Already there is a labor shortage.

Family Law

Due to the multi-ethnic nature of Singapore, family and inheritance laws are complex. The status of women varies according to the culture involved. The Women's Charter of 1961, which is based upon English common law, treats women's rights much the same as Western nations. But the Charter does not apply to Moslems. Polygyny to the extent of four wives is legal for Moslems as long as they comply with the requirements of Islamic law. In a marriage between a Moslem and a non-Moslem a couple may decide in advance whether Islamic or English common law will apply. In general women in Singapore have higher status than their sisters in other parts of Asia. They have equal rights in court, can vote, and own property. Many earn their own incomes.

Ethnic Indentity

Singapore is not a "melting pot" like the United States. Families of different ethnic groups share public housing and there is very little residential segregation. Yet, families socialize primarily within their own ethnic groups and there is little inter-marriage. Your Singapore business counterpart will have a definite cultural identity as an Indian, Malay, or Chinese. You will have to recognize such differences in your business dealings.

THE MALAY FAMILY

Birth

In Malay tradition the midwife spits on the baby to ward off the spirits of disease. She may press its skin with warm sireh leaves to welcome it to this world. This is followed by a recitation of Islamic beliefs and a call to prayer.

Forty-four days after birth a religious "naming" ceremony is held. Children are given Arabic names. The eldest son is often called "Awang" or "Long." The second son is named "Ngah," the third, "Alang." The naming ceremony is followed by a *kenduri,* a big feast. Gifts are appropriate at this time but must not include toy dogs.

Malays trace descent from the father but have no family surnames. A son will add *bin* (son of) and his father's given name to his own. A daughter will add *binti* (daughter of) in the same way.

Childhood

A Malay child is born with an economic disadvantage. Malays are less affluent than other ethnic groups in Singapore. Infant mortality is fairly high due to a diet heavy in starches. For this reason many mothers will nurse their babies for three years.

Malays raise their children with great tenderness and affection. Harsh words and blows are seldom used. They are allowed to learn first hand about fire and knives by burning and cutting themselves. Parents refuse to protect children from the realities of life by acting as authority figures. Instead, children learn through imitation of their parents.

There is little emphasis upon forcing a child to control its bladder and sphincter. Children below the age of one are often left naked below the waist. It is easier to clean the floor than clothes.

Older children are often assigned to look after younger siblings. The father takes an active role in raising children. At an early age they learn the concept of *budi,* which stresses respect, courtesy, harmony, and love. Boys are circumcized when they reach puberty. Tradition includes a limited form of female circumcision. Both are religious obligations.

Upbringing

Religious instruction begins with the Five Pillars of Islam: professing the unity of God, prayers five times daily, daylight fasts during the month of Ramadan, making the pilgrimage to Mecca, and giving part of one's assets to the poor. In addition, a Moslem is not supposed to eat pork, amphibians, or carnivors. Permitted meat must come from animals slaughtered in accordance with Islamic law. You may need such meat for a business dinner. It is packed for sale with a green star and crescent or the word *"halal"* on the package. Alcohol and gambling are proscribed.

To follow the precepts of Islam, Malay women must not wear immodest clothing. They must not touch men casually nor may they sit with them in the mosque. They are allowed to adorn themselves with much of their families' assets in the form of gold and jewels.

Courtship and Marriage

Malay women often marry while quite young. While a few marriages are still arranged, most Malays choose their own mates and then seek parental approval. The engagement begins when older members of the man's family visit the woman's family with gifts, dowry proposals, and a suggested wedding date. This visit is followed by a *kenduri,* attended by both families.

Malay weddings are colorful and musical. The bridal chamber is decorated with bright silks and satins. The marriage is performed by a man who is trained in Islamic law. Polygyny is allowed for Moslems but it is now rare. Only affluent Malays, which are also rare, can afford more than one wife. The divorce rate is high. A Moslem may divorce his wife by saying a *talak,* "I divorce you." His reasons may seem trivial, such as joking with men. One or two *talak* create a divorce in which the couple must live apart for one hundred days. If the husband does not cancel the divorce the woman is free to marry. If he announces a third *talak* the divorce is final. The couple may remarry only if the ex-wife first re-marries and divorces another man. There have been rare instances where a Malay husband, wanting his wife back, has paid a very poor old man to marry and quickly divorce her.

Death

When a Malay dies his body is covered with a white cloth and his head is positioned facing Mecca. Mourning is restrained. Friends bring flowers and money in white envelopes and passages from the Koran are read. The body is buried on its right side with its face in the direction of Mecca. Two planks, one over and one under the body, are used instead of a coffin. The soul goes to Allah to await the day of judgment.

The Individual

What kind of an individual does the Malay family system produce? While he or she may not follow all the traditions listed here, there remains a strong influence from the past. A Malay is a communal person who believes that life is a rapidly passing experience in which people are more important than possessions. Love and sharing are stressed. Life is easy and graceful. It only reluctantly involves the bustle of business.

THE INDIAN FAMILY

Birth

Until recent generations infant mortality was very high among Singapore's Indians. So concern with the survival of the child has carried over to the present. Indian parents, following tradition, consider the first twenty days of life to be critical. During this period there are many restrictions on the mother and child. On the twenty-eighth day after birth the baby is considered to be out of danger and is named. It is placed on its father's lap and its name is whispered into its ear.

Upbringing

An Indian child is raised to have a self-concept as a family unit. Within the family there is a rich, variegated tradition which allows a child to choose from many behavioral patterns. All stress a natural upbringing which socializes the child without destroying its spontaneity.

Courtship and Marriage

Young Indians usually meet in groups. In traditional families single dating is discouraged. Indian parents still have some influence over the marriage choices of their offspring. Engagement ceremonies are usually held at the girl's home and attended by the young man's relatives. After the engagement the couple is free to date but their behavior must be proper.

At the wedding ceremony the couple plants a small tree in a pot to symbolize their life together. They may be purified by walking around a holy fire. A *thali*, ceremonial necklace, is placed around the bride's neck and guests throw yellow rice, symbolic of fertility, at the couple. Some married women draw a red dot on their foreheads to mark their marriages.

Death

Indians believe the soul lingers awhile at the site of death. Oil lamps are lighted. The body is cleansed and dressed in new clothes. Silver coins are placed on the eyes. Floral wreaths, in muted colors, are sent to the home of the deceased person. Adults are usually cremated; the soul will find a new body. A widow will rub the red dot from her forehead and avoid the temple for a year.

THE CHINESE FAMILY

Birth

A child is considered one year old at birth. A year is added at each Chinese New Year. A special celebration is held one month after birth. For Chinese, it is essential that a couple have at least one male child. Couples will sometimes produce many daughters in hope of having a son. If many attempts fail, some couples will adopt a young boy, often a nephew, to carry on the family line.

Childhood

Young children are treated with great permissiveness and are included in every aspect of family life. Chinese children are usually not separated from the family by giving them their own rooms in childhood. Instead they sleep with their parents and become dependent upon them. Western parents will sometimes punish a child by keeping it in the house. In contrast Chinese parents may punish it by putting it outside.

Early childhood training emphasizes acceptance by the family and a natural, uninhibited upbringing. Respect for parents is instilled at an early age but children are never rejected or made to feel guilty. Chinese do not have puberty rites. A child is accepted as an important member of the family as soon as it is born.

Education

The days of permissiveness are over when a child enters school. The Chinese of Singapore have high academic achievement because to fail would cause parents to lose face. Confucius was, after all, a teacher. In schools in Singapore children are taught moral, political, and social values as well as standard academic subjects.

Courtship and Marriage

To start the engagement a young man offers special types of sweets, wrapped in red paper, to the young women's family and friends. Every effort is made to win over both families because the approval of parents and grandparents is highly desired. Rings or jewelry are often exchanged between the future bride and groom and a symbolic dowry is given to the woman's parents.

Chinese marriages involve much feasting and laughter. If you are invited to one it is a good idea to bring a gift of money, in even bills, in a red envelope.

Middle Age

Due to the stress on conformity individual personality may not bloom until middle age. Even then there may be considerable parental control. A Chinese woman's status improves markedly when a son marries, particularly if he brings his wife into his mother's household.

Old Age and Death

Old people are treated with great deference in Chinese society. They remain important family members even when they become too old to participate in work or decision-making. The Chinese practice which Westerners call "ancestor worship" is not really worship. It is instead, a public remembrance of ancestors. For Chinese the past flows into the present, forming a timeless fount to nurture the future. Something not forgotten cannot die.

Deaths are commemorated with long, elaborate ceremonies. A wake is held with much mourning. The body is carried to the cemetery or crematorium on a lavishly decorated truck displaying a photo of the deceased. Mourners wear sackcloth dyed in the color of death, white. Sometimes a brass band blares loudly. About a week after the funeral the family "air mails" essential items, such as houses, cars, and television sets to the deceased by burning paper replicas.

The Individual

What kind of person does the Chinese family system create?

To be Chinese is to conform. Family obligations come first. One must meet parental expectations and is not free to "do his own thing." Although this system is slowly modernizing, achievement, conformity, and discipline are still the hallmarks of the Chinese family.

Chinese are secular people. They have materialistic goals. Big houses and big cars seem to be particularly important to the Chinese of Singapore. They are willing to sacrifice for long periods to accumulate wealth. Such striving, goal-oriented people usually do well in business.

3. Knowing Your Counterpart: Politics and Law

The City-State

Singapore is one of the world's few city-states. A city-state is a small self-governing country primarily dependent upon the commercial activity of a single city. City-states were common in the ancient world and the Middle Ages. Athens and Venice were prime examples. By the nineteenth century most city-states were absorbed into larger nation-states. They lost their independence because they lacked sufficient populations to form large armies and had insufficient natural resources for large scale heavy industry. Today only a few survive: Monaco, San Marino, and Singapore.

Singapore's one attempt to combine into a nation-state with its neighbors was a failure. Singapore's federation with nearby Malay nations was unworkable primarily because the Malaysian members feared the economic and political power of Singapore's Chinese population. Throughout Southeast Asia local people often feel antipathy towards the more successful Chinese who have settled in their midst.

Culture and Government

In Asia culture exerts a predominate influence upon politics. There are considerable differences between Asian political systems based upon group consciousness and conformity and Western systems derived from concepts of inalienable individual rights. The political and social contracts involved in each system may be considered equally valid if all within a system agree.

Many Asians consider Western versions of freedom to be license. They are troubled by the absence of common standards and they consider much of the behavior of individual Westerners to be blatantly selfish. Asians prefer the conformity of their own traditions because they want a settled, harmonious society. In contrast many Westerners look at Asian harmony and see only drab conformity, a boring and depressing sameness which stifles individual expression and impedes creativity. One American expatriate electronics executive described Singapore as "dull, sanitized, the bland leading the bland." Your vision depends upon your values.

The 1994 caning of an American youth as punishment for graffiti vandalism represented a watershed in Singapore's attitude toward itself and the outside world. In the past Western protests, such as those by President Clinton, would have convinced Singapore to lift the punishment: the awe of Western success was just too overwhelming. But this time Singapore, looking at a United States plagued by graffiti, dope, AIDs, child pregnancy, welfare dependency, and street violence, felt secure about its own social and economic system. So it validated its own values by carrying out the punishment.

Asians also tend to be less concerned about legality than Westerners. The legal codes which Westerners value so highly are considered to be too remote and inflexible by many Asians. Most Asian nations, including Singapore, have incorporated Western legal concepts, such as constitutions, into their political structures. But in day to day living Asians are often ruled by oral traditions which are enforced by neighbors. The Malays of Singapore, for example, often disdain laws enforced by strangers. They prefer their *adat,* an unwritten system of rule based on centuries of village life. The "guided democracy" of Singapore is an amalgam of values which treads a fine line between traditional Chinese authoritarianism and Western representative democracy.

Political History

The political history of Singapore is closely intertwined with the person of Lee Kuan Yew, the country's dominant political figure.

After the British recovered Singapore at the end of World War II, they returned it to the status of a colony without consulting the local people. Britain's Special Branch took care of left wing political weeds so a crop of stable, middle-of-the-road politicians could grow without challenge.

Britain's post-war financial problems and rising Asian nationalism made it obvious that Britain would soon dissolve its Asian empire. Some thought Singapore might be ceded to the Republic of China, the only Asian victor of the war. Others expected the island to become part of an extended Malay nation. Few expected it to become an independent city-state.

In the mid-1950s Singapore was torn by riots and strikes over unemployment, low wages, poor housing, and inadequate education. The British saw little to gain by keeping the colony. In 1956 Britain promised internal self-government to Singapore in 1959.

By the end of 1957 Lee Kuan Yew's group had achieved a dominant political position. It did so by maintaining a revolutionary anti-British posture while simultaneously receiving British support and patronage. Upon independence from Britain in 1959 Lee Kuan Yew and his People's Action Party won control through election. They have been in power ever since.

In 1961 the People's Action Party rejected its communist elements. Some of the reds formed the Barisan Socialis Party while others went underground. Since then very little serious political opposition has been tolerated. Some opposition leaders have been jailed. Some opposition presses have been closed. To Singapore's Chinese leaders there is no such thing as a "loyal opposition." One who opposes cannot be loyal. Disrespect to the leader may be tantamount to treason even if one feels much loyalty to the country.

In 1963 Lee Kuan Yew brought Singapore into the Federation of Malaysia which included Malaya, Sarawak, and Sabah. He thought there would be greater security and opportunity for Singapore in the federation. Instead, it faced the wrath of Sukarno of Indonesia, who disliked Chinese, and the fears of Malaysians concerning economic dominance by Singapore's Chinese majority. In addition Malay leaders viewed Singapore's large Chinese population as a political threat because the rebels in Malaya's guerilla war were mostly Chinese. Within two years the federation fell apart and Singapore was on its own again.

In 1985 an amendment to the Singapore Constitution extended government intolerance of opposition to Singapore citizens living abroad. This provision deprives Singaporeans of their citizenship if they reside abroad more than ten years continuously. This law effectively eliminated the challenge of expatriate dissidents.

On September 3, 1988, Lee's party won a landslide. Lee immediately announced that he would resign, concluding thirty years as prime minister. But Goh Chok Tong, his designated successor was elected prime minister.

Constitution and Governmental Structure

The Constitution of Singapore established a seventy-nine member parliament which is elected by secret ballot. Members serve for five years unless parliament is dissolved earlier. The parliament elects a prime minister and president. The president serves as head of state. The prime minister exercises executive power with a twelve-member cabinet.

Like many other political systems, Singapore's favors politicians already in power. There is a parliamentary system which gives *extra* seats to the party which gets the most votes. In the 1984 election the People's Action Party won seventy-seven out of seventy-nine seats although it had only sixty-three per cent of the popular vote. In the 1988 election the People's Action Party won all but one seat.

Sharing of power in the economic realm has been much more successful. The government has wisely delegated much authority to specialized agencies. In comparison to similar agencies in other countries these exercise unusual autonomy and flexibility.

Many of these agencies are listed in the chapters "How to Get Help" and "Useful Addresses." Some agencies you are likely to be involved with include the Economic Development Board and the Trade Development Board which provide assistance to foreigners interested in investment and trade opportunities. The National Productivity Board develops productivity policies and trains managers for better performance. The National Wages Council sets wages through equal representation from labor, management, and government. Jurong Town Corporation manages industrial estates. Others include the Public Utilities Board and the Monetary Authority. In Singapore there is a board or council for almost every economic activity.

Civil Rights?

Many Asians feel that the West has given up its old values and has been unable to find new ones. The government of Singapore is determined not to make the same mistake. The determination of good and bad follows precepts of "right conduct" established by China's ancient sages as interpreted by Lee Kuan Yew and his People's Action Party.

Conformity is the hallmark. People with long hair are sometimes forced to get haircuts. Foreign "hippies" are expelled. Beggars are required to learn a trade.

There are draconian fines for minor offenses, flogging and death for others. One may be fined for jaywalking, smoking on elevators or buses, littering, spitting, and leaving stagnant water (in which mosquitoes breed) under potted plants. Under certain conditions fines may be imposed for wearing long hair or chewing gum. The Clean Public Toilets Law, passed in 1989, inflicts penalties up to five hundred dollars for failing to flush toilets in restaurants, theaters, and department stores. This law is enforced by health officials who keep an eye on people using toilets. This purge has resulted in a steady stream of fines and a sharp increase in Singapore's importation of expensive water.

People who cannot pay the fines spend three months in Changi Prison, a former Japanese concentration camp. Those who commit more serious crimes are caned with rattan rods, a punishment not native but established by the British during the days of imperialism. Drug dealers are quickly executed. If you are scheduled to be hanged for a narcotics offense, arrangements can be made to mail your return air tickets to your next of kin so they can get a refund.

Pornography is outlawed. The government censors movies, radio, television, and all printed media. There are no negative role models for young people. Several magazines, including *Time,* were restricted in circulation for refusing to print government rebuttals to editorials in full text.

Motor vehicles also have no right against self-incrimination. Trucks must have roof lights which blink when the driver exceeds the speed limit. Cars have musical chimes for the same purpose. One's vehicle becomes a police informant.

While much of this seems oppressive by Western standards, there is a positive side. The island nation is clean and green. Pride follows appearance. Health, safety, and economic standards are high. There is virtually no homelessness, poverty, unemployment, drugs, or gang violence. Even *toy* guns are banned. Some observers describe this benevolent paternalism as a "velvet trap."

As a visitor to Singapore you should not become involved in its politics. The government is very sensitive to criticism by foreigners. You need to learn how the political system works because you will be dealing with it. As an investor you have a right to assess political risk.

Political Prospects

Although Singapore has had one-party rule for over thirty years, the government has been efficient and graft free. Standards are high. In your dealings with government officials do not even give the appearance of offering bribes. This government is not likely to fall from corruption.

There has been little opportunity for input of opposing views in the development of government policy. Yet its decisions have been generally wise and workable. This government is unlikely to fall from mismanagement.

Future political problems are most likely to result from changing world economic conditions. As an entrepot Singapore is more dependent upon world trade than most economies. A deep world recession could bring serious social and racial discord. Like pancake make-up, prosperity hides many blemishes.

Like Taiwan, South Korea, and China, Singapore is struggling to reconcile an authoritarian political tradition with the demands of a modern economy. A growing flexible business class is becoming increasingly restless with rigid government constraints. As recent events in China show, a conflict between a free market economy and a hierarchical government can create risks for Western businesses. Fiats and Fiats don't mix!

PART TWO

Business and Economy

Singapore has one of the fastest growing economies in the world. This success is due primarily to its ability to build export business, act as an entrepot, develop high technology, and function as a regional base for international corporations.

In order to operate successfully in Singapore you will need to understand how its economy developed, how it functions, and its strengths and weaknesses. This section will also help you with some of the practical problems of doing business. These topics include information on how to get help in doing business in Singapore, standards of commercial etiquette, and techniques for business negotiation.

As we look at the business and economic environment in Singapore we should keep in mind the cultural and social foundations already covered. Business people are people first. As such, culture is a primary determinant of behavior.

4. A Brief Economic History of Singapore

Location for Trade

For an island only thirteen miles north to south and twenty-seven miles east to west Singapore has played an unusually prominent role in world trade. This has been largely due to its location off the southern tip of the Malay Peninsula. As indicated on the map at the back of this book the island is situated astride the narrowest portion of the sea lane between the Strait of Malacca and the South China Sea. Ships steaming the shortest route between Japan or China and the Indian Ocean must pass through this channel. The island also benefits from a brisk trade in regional production of spices, oil, rubber, and tin.

Although Singapore's location is favorable its climate is not. Without the presence of man the inhospitable heat and humidity would bring back its ancient blanket of tropical rain forests and mangrove swamps.

Early Economy

The early Malays maintained a simple economy. They lived by and from the sea and engaged in fishing, trade, and piracy. About 300 B.C. these early stone-age Malays were pushed inland by a stronger group of Malays which arrived with iron weapons and tools. These new Malays also lived from the sea. But they had more intense agriculture. Since

39

planting and harvesting could only be done during short periods timed to the vagaries of the monsoons the entire community had to participate. This led to a communal system of work and property ownership.

The same monsoons that watered Malay crops carried Malay sea traders to Southeast Asia. Indeed, the word *"monsoon"* is Arabic for season. The seasonal winds called monsoons made possible a trade in spices, lumber, foodstuffs, and handicrafts. Great trading empires developed. By the thirteenth century the Indianized Malay Kingdom of Sri Vijaya controlled commerce between India, the Middle East, Africa, and Southeast Asia. By the end of the century a prince of this maritime power built a port city on the island of Singapore.

In time Singapore was invaded by Mongols and overrun by pirates. Trade was disrupted. The city was abandoned and sank into oblivion. Soon only a few fishermen and farmers squatted amid its brooding ruins.

The Arrival of the British

The modern history of Singapore began with Sir Stamford Raffles. Raffles was a self-made man who began his business career at the age of fourteen as a clerk for the East India Company. During his five month voyage to Penang in 1805 Raffles studied and mastered the Malay language. Once he arrived at Penang he immersed himself in the culture. Later, on Java, he used his spare time to write a definitive history of the island. On his first return to England he carried thirty tons of museum quality specimens and artifacts. While his competitors played cricket Raffles studied the languages, geography, culture, arts, history, and politics of the region. His intellectual curiosity produced big profits. Today many international firms recognize the example of Raffles when they recruit people who know foreign languages and cultures. For business, like all human activity, is primarily a social science.

In 1819 Raffles visited Singapore and decided to develop it as a free port to counter Dutch trade in nearby Malaya. Raffles leased Singapore by supporting a minor Sultan, Tunku Long. Within hours Raffles started clearing the 160 million year old rain forest. Within days he was constructing a fort and port. Within a week Singapore was in business. Great Britain now had a strategic trading post midway on the sea route between Calcutta and Canton. Ships of all nations came to replenish food and water, make repairs, and trade. It was the commercial coup of the century.

The Dutch responded by agreeing to a treaty recognizing British control of Singapore and Malaya in return for British recognition of Dutch interests in Java and Sumatra. This one act created a division of Malay people, culture, and language which still persists.

Britain had acquired the island of Penang in 1786. With the addition of the city of Malacca, the three cities-Malacca, Penang, and Singapore—became known as the British Straits Settlements. Thus was derived the usage of the term "Straits" for names of today's newspapers and stock indexes in Singapore.

Singapore began as a business venture and it boomed from the beginning. Raffles had perceived that Asia was about to undergo a vast transformation. As Japan, then other nations, felt the adrenalin of modernization, regional trade expanded and Singapore's fortunes soared.

Raffles had obtained Singapore by taking advantage of Malay factionalism. The British claimed the Malays welcomed them so they could "set the troubled Malay house in order." But this claim was belied by a series of revolts against the British. The Perak War, Negri Sembilan War, Selangor War, Pahang Rebellion, and Kelantan Rising kept Malaya in turmoil. When the leader of the Kelantan Rising, To' Jangguf, was hanged his body was suspended upside down and left to rot in a public square. British ships, cannon, and gallows smothered the movement for Malay independence but it smoldered for over a century. The winds of World War II finally whipped it into flames.

Economic Development under the British

British rule brought modern factories, banks, waterworks, roads, railways, printing presses, post offices, telegraphs, telephones, and schools. Health standards were improved. A smallpox vaccine was developed from the lymph of water buffalo. But Britain's best benefits were political stability and free trade. Singapore became a magnet which attracted business people from suppressed areas of Asia, where monarchical regulations, state monopolies, exorbitant taxes, and extortion by capricious officials stifled the entrepreneurial spirit.

As China suffered "the death of a thousand cuts" under the knives of Western imperialists more Chinese moved to Singapore. Many from coastal provinces already had experience with seaborne trade. But the largest influx of Chinese came with the opening of tin mines and rubber plantations in nearby Malaya. Since the Malays were not willing to work such long hours, the British imported Indian laborers. The newly arrived Chinese provided retail services and trade to the burgeoning towns of Indian workers. In time some Chinese became mine and plantation overseers and owners. Chinese merchants also became the middlemen for trade in local export crops. They soon dominated Singapore's construction industry, docks, and mills. The success of the Chinese made many Malay people jealous and resentful. This feeling is still an important factor in the politics of the island.

The mines and plantations were very profitable. Tin cans had first been used by Napoleon's army in 1808; by the mid-nineteenth century they were in common use. By this time there was also a brisk demand for tin for corrugated roofing and a need for rubber for rain protection and carriage tires.

As the region's economy boomed it attracted droves of Indian laborers, mostly Tamils from the south. They were paid subsistence wages so they would remain dependent on their jobs. Sikhs, working as company police, kept discipline with beatings. The illiterate, underfed, and abused Indian workers slept in huge dormitories, often with no mattresses. During recessions when work was scarce, they were thrown off the land.

The Europeans of Singapore, not all British, contributed business skills, capital, and technology. Giant dredges, industrial dinosaurs, wallowed in the mining ponds, chewing chunks of tin from the mud. Millions of rubber saplings from Brazil sprouted on Malaya's west coast. Most Malays refused to become involved in the brutal new technology. But the Chinese in Singapore benefited from the region's new economic efficiency.

With the advent of steamships in the 1860s Singapore became a great trading center which collected and processed raw materials such as Malayan rubber and tin, Sumatran oil, Vietnamese coal, and gold from Luzon. As the city collected these commodities it distributed European manufactured products. The opening of the Suez Canal in 1869 tripled Singapore's shipping tonnage within three years. By the close of the nineteenth century Singapore was the most polygot city in Asia. Chinese, Indians, Javanese, Filipinos, Malayans, Sumatrans and Europeans shared a common purpose: making money.

World War I benefited Malaya and Singapore by increasing the demand for rubber and tin. After the war the rubber industry earned most of the dollars Britain needed to repay war loans to the United States. By this time the United States, emerging from the war as the world's greatest economic power, was consuming most of the world's rubber and tin production.

As a colony highly dependent upon world trade Singapore was hit particularly hard by the Great Depression of the 1930s. By 1932 unemployment was so high the country stopped male immigration. On the eve of World War II a recovering Singapore was processing and shipping forty per cent of the world's rubber and sixty per cent of its tin.

Japanese Conquest

As an increasingly powerful Japan invaded Manchuria and China in the 1930s Britain moved to protect Singapore. British naval experts expected any threat to the island to come from the sea. So in 1938 the British established the Royal Naval Base and stored an underground supply of food and ammunition sufficient for a sixty-day siege. This was considered enough time for the invincible British navy to steam to the rescue of Singapore. The island was never fortified against land attack because the jungle to the north was considered impenetrable.

It was unfortunate that all major gun emplacements rigidly faced the sea. When the Japanese attack came it was from the north down the Malaya coast. The Royal Navy, busy in the Mediterranean, never reached the area in strength. A token force, consisting of the *Repulse* and *Prince of Wales,* arrived but was sunk by Japanese planes. When the Japanese army arrived within sight of Singapore the government was still urging its people to plant gardens for a long siege. British artillery was negotiating with a golf course manager for permission to set up on fairways. On February 15, 1942, the garrison of 130,000 troops surrendered to a Japanese army half its size.

Under the supervision of the dreaded Kempei Tai (Secret Police) General Yamashita's army massacred five thousand Chinese. Many were bound and thrown in Singapore Harbor. Others were buried alive or machine gunned on the beaches. Under the fire of Japanese artillery the City of Lions had become a jumble of broken water mains and collapsed buildings. Many hospitals and food stores closed. Disease, malnutrition, and poverty became the common lot. The Japanese renamed Singapore *Syonan,* "Brilliant South." Crippled and shell gutted, the island staggered through the war.

The fall of Singapore punctured the myth of white racial superiority upon which Western imperialism was largely dependent. Asians had seen the Japanese use European prisoners for bayonet practice to show that white skin was not inviolate. The white man had been beaten. The fall of Singapore helped produce postwar independence movements in Asia. The West would no longer be able to force its will.

Postwar Economy

The end of World War II brought an immediate demand for rubber, tin, spices, palm oil, and timber. At first the economy of Singapore boomed. As nearby nations began to build their own processing plants and ports, Singapore shifted from regional to international trade. The outbreak of the Korean War in 1950 greatly stimulated the island's economy.

Japan's emergence as a world economic power in the late 1950s gave it a thirst for oil. Singapore was ideally located to refine Arab oil on the way to Japan. In 1959 Singapore offered "pioneer" tax incentives to international oil companies for constructing refineries. Thus one of the first economic policy decisions of the newly independent nation was to encourage foreign investment. This policy was to produce great success in future years.

The end of the British Empire and Singapore's exclusion from the Malaysian Federation in 1965 produced economic problems. In response the government developed labor intensive manufacturing for export and import substitution. This was achieved by targeting "pioneer" industries for special tax and financial incentives. Singapore offered greater incentives for foreign investment than any other Asian nation.

As the nation came to full employment industrial policy produced a shift from labor intensive to capital intensive industry. During the war in Vietnam vast infusions of capital developed Singapore's shipyards, repair shops, oil refineries, chemical and machinery industries. The logistical and material requirements of the war were huge and Singapore was nearby.

The government met each new problem with great success. One occurred with the closing of Britain's naval base in 1970. Another was produced by rising prices of Japanese goods in 1972. In the mid-1970s the first Arab oil shock quadrupled the price of oil and sharply reduced the island's income. The government met these crises by expanding Singapore's role as a regional corporate and financial center. It did this by expanding the Asian Dollar Market, eliminating exchange controls, and offering additional tax inducements to foreign corporations.

In 1985 and early 1986 the economy again declined. The government formed an economic committee which concluded that the economy had become too socialized and needed a dose of supply side economics. The government reduced personal and corporate taxes, loosened requirements for corporate contributions to social security funds, and instituted wage restraints. Singapore's firms once again regained their competitive positions in the world economy. By 1990 Singapore had become a global high-tech player, fully capable of competing in the information age.

5. A Look at Singapore's Successful Economy

An Economic Miracle

Singapore's economic miracle has enabled it to tie Taiwan as the nation with the second highest standard of living in Asia. Japan is first. Singapore's per capita gross national product exceeds ten thousand dollars.

In some ways Singapore's quality of life is better than Japan's. The city's emerald parks, broad beaches and open scenery create a spacious elegance which contrasts favorably with the polluted industry and cramped residential warrens of Japan.

Singapore's miniature miracle has managed to succeed in business without creating an underclass mired in poverty. There are no homeless. Half the population lives in low rent or government assisted housing. The government encourages home ownership. Health, sanitation, and recreation standards approximate those in the west. Education is in some ways better.

Reasons for Success

Singapore has no important mineral or agricultural assets. Its domestic market is small. So what accounts for its success?

The government formula which created Singapore's vibrant economy includes investment in people, incentives for business and free trade policies. The government recognized early that people were Singapore's most valuable assets. A big effort went into a system of free and effective education. It taught positive behavior and attitudes as well as knowledge and skills. Non-religious moral values were emphasized in a way last seen in the United States in the 1940s. The result is a highly educated citizenry which works hard, saves money, and accepts civic responsibility.

The island's economic planners used fiscal and monetary policies to good effect. Rather than "priming the pump" through deficit spending and bloating the money supply the government budgeted for a surplus and kept the supply and demand for money in balance. The surplus was used to finance industry and infrastructure.

Industrial policy first centered upon the island's role as an entrepot, then on import substitution, labor intensive manufacturing, capital intensive industry, high-tech manufacturing, and ultimately international finance and regional corporate headquarters activities. The small size of Singapore made centralized government planning more effective than in larger nations. Every time economic conditions changed the government was ready with a new policy.

Singapore encouraged foreign investment more than any other nation in Asia. A system of financial incentives for "pioneer" industries created many new businesses and much new employment. Government corporate ownership was usually limited to temporary equity investment rather than direct operation.

As the first free port of modern times Singapore set the example for Hong Kong and shows how the world will benefit when all national trade barriers are removed.

Much of Singapore's commercial and economic development was financed through private savings. A savings rate of about forty per cent is enforced through required deposits to the Central Provident Fund, which employees may use to buy a public housing unit or retire at fifty-five.

A final factor in Singapore's economic success is the government's ability to keep the public informed about the realities of world economics: why wages must be limited, how resources must be prioritized, and why savings and foreign investment are required. This effective campaign of public information has kept costs competitive and attracted much foreign investment.

Infrastructure

The government ensures efficient use of the island's limited ground space by locating housing, transportation, and commercial sites in a way designed to expedite commuting and preserve the appearance of the city. Such planning guided the construction of ports, airports, highways, power utilities, and telecommunications facilities. The land area of the island was expanded by two of the world's largest landfills in the harbor.

Telegraph, telephone, and postal systems are modern and efficient. Singapore is the largest user of satellite communications in Southeast Asia with over six hundred international circuits. Some seventy-seven post offices serve the island. Local Urgent Mail is delivered within two hours of collection.

The transportation system is extensive. Expressways link the New Town residential areas with the city center. The Mass Rapid Transit System, a combination of underground and above ground rail transport will soon have the capacity for a million rides per day. The island is linked to Malaya by a causeway which carries both a road and railroad. At the new airport at Changi more than forty airlines serve over ten million passengers per year. Singapore Airlines is the world's seventh largest and flies mostly three-year old Boeings. The port, which operates around the clock, is the world's second busiest. It can load ninety containers per hour. One ship leaves port every nine minutes.

The Public Utilities Board manages Singapore's electric, gas, and water utilities. These efficient and dependable systems serve all parts of Singapore. High quality industrial water is available at economical rates.

Basic Industries

The Jurong Town Corporation, established in 1968, constructs fully equipped manufacturing facilities which are leased or sold to corporations at reasonable prices. Its parks account for almost three-quarters of Singapore's manufacturing production. Certain of its industrial estates are designated for specific industries: the Southern Islands for petrochemicals, Sungei Kadut and Kranji for wood products, Loyang and Seletar for aviation manufacturing. Land rents vary from roughly five dollars to thirty dollars per square meter per year.

In recent years Singapore's economy has become more sophisticated through expansion of the petrochemical plant at Pulau Ayer Merhau and the development of facilities to produce state of the art computer systems, circuit boards, and electronics office equipment. Major semiconductor companies have chosen Singapore as the site for fabrication of the new generation of wafers.

The commercial section of the United States Embassy has identified the following industries as attractive for investment and sales: electronic products and test equipment, aviation and avionics support equipment, computers, office equipment, machine tools, metalworking equipment, medical instruments, health care equipment, tourism, biotechnology, consumer products, and food.

Foreign Trade

The following nations account for two-thirds of Singapore's trade: Japan, the United States, Malaysia, the People's Republic of China, and the countries of the European Economic Community. By product two-thirds of Singapore's trade involves petroleum, electronic products, machinery and transport equipment, and basic commodities such as rubber and timber.

Tourism

Singapore is clean, green, and safe. Its fine hotels, parks, and beaches attract about 3.5 million tourists per year. English is widely spoken. For non-English speakers there are over five hundred licensed tour guides speaking a total of twenty-six languages. The city is one of few in Asia where it is safe to drink tap water.

Singapore is one big shopping center which attracts bargain seekers from all over the world. The seventy-three story Westin Stamford, the tallest hotel in Asia, incorporates a gigantic convention center.

Banking and Finance

The Monetary Authority of Singapore is responsible for the management of Singapore's financial system. The Board of Commissioners of Currency is responsible for currency issue and redemption. The Singapore dollar, recently valued at roughly sixty-eight cents, is a stable currency which is loosely linked to the United States dollar.

Singapore operates a twenty-four hour per day, worldwide market involving stocks, bonds, options, and commodities. Its location makes transactions with both Europe and the United States possible within a single day. Some three hundred banks, insurance companies, and brokerages make Singapore the Switzerland of Southeast Asia. There are three types of commercial banks: fully licensed, restricted, and offshore. Restricted banks may not offer savings accounts, receive small deposits, or operate more than one branch. Branches of foreign banks are usually restricted. Offshore banks specialize in wholesale banking with foreigners.

There are many specialized government and private financial institutions. Merchant banks specialize in investment banking. Discount houses invest short-term money. The Development Bank of Singapore finances new and existing factories. International money brokers, insurance, and finance companies perform functions similar to their counterparts in the United States.

Research and Technology

The government is currently restructuring the economy to place more emphasis upon high-tech, high-skill industries. Singapore's role as a center for international technology is being expanded by the continued development of such industries as automation, robotics, aerospace, communications, and electronics. In the past Singapore has been primarily dependent upon foreign corporations for research and development. It is now working to develop its own capabilities in these areas.

Education

Singapore's commercial success is largely due to the government's investment in education and the high educational expectations parents have for their children. The educational system is so competitive that college bound secondary school students average nearly five hours of homework per day. This leaves students little time to balance study with recreation, music, or sports. Such high educational standards have contributed to the Lion City's roaring success. Several businessmen told me that, when hiring Americans, they need to hire college graduates to do jobs which require only a local high school education.

The government recognizes that an educated elite is not enough to maintain a modern economy. Such institutions as Nanyang Technical Institute, Singapore Polytech, and Ngee Ann Polytech emphasize training of technicians at all levels.

Management

Singapore now has so many skilled managers it provides them to businesses in other nations of the region. International corporations find they can put a Singaporean management into Indonesia or Malaya for about one hundred thousand dollars per year. This is less than half the cost of assigning an American or European to a similar position. These Singaporean expatriates usually have a better feel for the local culture than Westerners.

A Haven?

Singapore's success is likely to be enhanced by its role as a haven in a trouble region of the world. The 1989 massacres of freedom demonstrators in Beijing resulted in the diversion of some trade and investment to Singapore. For the same reason many Chinese in Hong Kong plan to leave the colony before it reverts to China in 1997. Singapore's employees are advertising in Hong Kong papers to attract engineers, architects, medical and computer specialists, foreign exchange traders, and student pilots. The government of Singapore is offering relocation assistance and permanent residence status to these professionals. Much of the skilled human resources of Hong Kong will probably end up in Singapore.

Amid all this business euphoria it should be remembered that nothing is more vulnerable than entrenched success. Singapore has its share of problems. We will look at some of them in the next chapter.

6. Current Problems

Types of Problems

Singapore has achieved economic success in spite of a variety of problems. These difficulties are related to rising United States protectionism, dependence upon the world economy, defense costs, size limitations, problems of identify, labor and social unrest, and the challenge of adjusting its political system to a changing world economy.

Rising United States Protectionism

The United States is Singapore's largest customer and second largest supplier next to Japan. The United States accounts for roughly twenty-three per cent of Singapore's exports.

In recent years there have been both economic and political strains in Singapore's relations with the United States. In May, 1988, E. Mason Hendrickson, the First Secretary of the United States Embassy, was expelled from Singapore after accusations of aiding the government's political opposition. In retaliation the United States expelled Hendrickson's Singaporean counterpart in Washington. This resulted in a government sponsored demonstration against the United States by four thousand people in Singapore.

Singapore's reluctance to enforce copyright laws has also created problems with the United States. The island's censors effectively block the import of video cassettes which they find to be morally and politically objectionable. But they are unable to block trade in pirated cassettes which violate international copyrights.

Dependence upon the World Economy

Singapore, as a trading nation, is unusually dependent upon world economic conditions which are outside its control. Decisions made in Tokyo, Washington, and London affect its commerce. International corporations, which produce a quarter of the nation's gross national product, have limited allegiance to the island. Due to its lack of resources Singapore's economy is unusually vulnerable to minor swings in commodity prices. Large price increases in commodities such as copper, timber, oil, or rubber could wreak economic havoc similar to the oil shocks of the 1970s. On the other hand sharp price decreases in such commodities would be the result of low demand. The reduction in trading volume in regionally produced commodities helped produce Singapore's 1985-86 recession.

Defense Costs

The recent turmoil in China could cause its government to pursue a policy of military expansion designed to detract attention from its domestic problems. This would have profound implications for the nations of Southeast Asia. Singapore would have to increase its defense spending. Paradoxically the island would have some help from a growing Japanese navy, which has set itself the mission of keeping Singapore's straits open for Japan's vital oil imports from the Middle East.

Size Limitations

Singapore's small size sets inherent limitations upon its economic development. Rising consumer expectations have caused space problems. Most Singaporeans want cars. But the highways and streets have limited capacity. So the government severely restricts traffic in the downtown area and imposes taxes which raise the prices of imported cars. A

Honda costs roughly thirty-eight thousand dollars. A Hyundai sells for twenty-three thousand.

The island has limited room for immigrants. The government is trying to attract highly trained professionals from Hong Kong while discouraging the immigration of untrained workers from Malaya, Thailand, and Indonesia. In a recent amnesty ten thousand illegal residents from Thailand returned home, but many remain. A tough law provides three months in jail and three strokes of the cane for illegal residents. Attempts to implement this law have resulted in threats to Singapore's embassy and airline offices in Bangkok. The government has tried to increase the room for people by building high rise housing developments on land reclaimed from cemeteries. But older superstitious Singaporeans refuse to live in "burial houses."

Singapore plans to compensate for its small size by establishing industrial parks abroad. In a joint venture with Jiangsu Province of China, Singapore is developing a twenty-seven square mile industrial zone in Suzhou, near Shanghai.

The Problem of Identity

A country needs to have a deeper meaning than shopping.

Singapore's colorful past is literally buried in shopping centers and high-rise hotels. Gone are the swarms of beetle backed bumboats from the harbor. Gone are the viand vendors which once crowded Chinatown's narrow alleys. Gone are the turbaned snake charmers and their lethargic, defanged companions. The sing song sounds of Chinese outdoor operas no longer rise from Orchard Road. It is hard to find a mosque or temple amid the mass of myriad modern buildings. Singapore's authentic Asian clutter has been replaced with sanitary order. The neutral scents of modern air fresheners conceal its venerable odors. No soul.

By the mid-1980s Western visitors in search of authentic Asian textures were finding only smooth, modern tedium.

They were not impressed by big modern hotels. Tourism declined dramatically.

Singapore's Tourist Promotion Board and Urban Redevelopment Authority responded to this problem by beginning the renovation of a large area in the heart of the city, including the Raffles Hotel. These planners are trying to avoid the creation of a plastic oriental theme park. Slowly the resurrection of the old city's opulent structures takes shape. Some bumboats are back and tourists are returning.

Labor and Social Problems

In some ways the government of Singapore is performing a risky balancing act on thin wire. Local politics requires increased social spending for housing, health, and education. Yet such expenditures raise the island's costs of doing business and reduce its international competitive position.

At times the island's militant labor unions have reduced profitability by pushing up labor costs. Singapore's manufacturing wages are now higher than those in Korea, Hong Kong, and Taiwan. Asia's labor intensive industry is moving to low-wage nations such as Thailand, Sri Lanka, and Bangladesh. Already many of Singapore's textile, footwear, food, and beverage plants have made the move.

After some labor strife the government established the National Wages Council (1972) and reactivated the National Productivity Board (1980). Both try to keep increases in wages and benefits in line with improvements in productivity. Few nations of the world have been able to succeed without a common language and culture. Singapore is a potpourri of races, cultures, and religions. It is not a melting pot. Its independence in 1959 was greeted with racial and labor strife. Hostilities between the Chinese majority and Indian and Malay minorities still smolder. Riots similar to those involving the Bertha Hertogh case in 1950 and the Malay-Chinese incidents in 1964 can occur at any time. A future political, economic, or social crisis could again bring violence. Resurgent Islamic fundamentalism could produce serious problems. So far the government has maintained a tenuous working relationship with Chinese, Malays, and Indians. It takes many political trade offs and copious applications of balmy salves of success to keep this little island stable.

Traditional Politics versus the New Economics

Centralized political power and a decentralized market economy are basically incompatible. No nation can long maintain a free market economy without the political freedoms free market economies create. When the fresh blood of private commercial enterprise courses through sclerotic political arteries something has to give.

Power follows money. The process of economic decentralization which makes a nation economically successful inevitably dilutes the power of authoritarian government. Economic competition leads always to political diversity.

Mankind is entering an age of communication in which a major portion of a nation's economic assets must be distilled from free flowing information. Billions of bytes, too many to censor, stream through wires or satellite microwaves and instantaneously penetrate national borders. The nervous system of the New Age economy, consisting of computer circuits, modems, minicams, cellular phones, and VCRs, has no regard for the propaganda of parliaments, presidents, or politburos. No power in the world can separate facts from faxs.

Governments which try to maintain strong centralized control find themselves operating at a disadvantage in this gyrating business environment. A nation's political and economic systems must both enter the new information age or neither will. In some Asian nations the brittle conservatism of the old political order has produced stagnant economies, social unrest, brain drains, and the flight of essential capital.

Singapore's government is more flexible than many. But it prefers placid political waters at a time the whole world is being swept into the turbulent vortex of a new capitalistic economic revolution.

Transition of Leadership

Most of the nations of the East Asian rim have more challenging educational systems, better work ethics, and higher savings rates than the United States. Yet in the recipe for modern economies, many lack an essential ingredient: a process for peaceful change of power between opposition political parties. It is difficult to name an example of an Asian ruling party peacefully surrendering power after free elections. These governments do not walk away from power like their Western counterparts. Instead they cling to power long after they are moribund. What appears to be stability is too often stagnation.

A nation cannot be sure it has a democratic system until there has been a peaceful change of power between opposing parties. This simple process, so routine in the West, is the acid test of democracy. Most nations of Asia have never met it. Singapore has not.

Yet many nations of East Asia have successful economies without Western style democracies. So why should the development of democratic political systems be important? They are important because the dynamics of today's revolutionary world information economy require frequent government policy changes which can best be met by flexible, multi-party political systems. Only periodic rotation of power can create openings for new ideas, accommodate new generations, and facilitate fresh adjustments to rapidly changing economic realities. The modern world is so complicated that no one party can provide all the answers and solve all the problems.

Many Asians criticize the United States as being near political anarchy. But they overlook the innate stability of our system. The Great Depression of the 1930s produced such human suffering that it could have caused a revolution in the United States. It did not because the American people knew they would have an opportunity to produce a change of government in a free election. Asians tacitly recognize this stability because many move their assets into dollars every time they have a political crisis.

Although you must not become involved in Singapore's politics, you do have a responsibility to assess your political risk. A look at recent history forces the conclusion that most Asian nations lack the democratic tools needed to deal with severe crises. When these occur the long delayed shifts in power come suddenly and violently. The standard procedure for change of power between opposition parties in Asia involves riots, coups, assassinations, and revolutions. This political brittleness seems to be the one major flaw in Asia's ability to compete in the new world economy. Until Singapore shows it can pass power peacefully between parties it will remain vulnerable to the possibility its glittering economic miracle could end in whiffs of riot gas.

7. Doing Business in Singapore

Opportunities

Why do business in Singapore? American business people on the island cite various reasons. Singapore is an attractive base for an Asian corporate headquarters because people speak English; it is less costly than Tokyo or Taipei and it does not have the political problems of Hong Kong. Singapore offers manufacturing corporations well trained labor at reasonable wages. For traders it offers a free port. For international financiers the island provides a location which bridges the time gap between business hours of major world stock exchanges. Finally, the government actively encourages foreign trade and investment.

Getting Started

To get started one might enlist the help of banks and government agencies in the United States and Singapore. Chapter Nine explains how these function. Chapter Thirteen lists addresses. You should write for appointments several months in advance because business people in Singapore frequently travel. Confirm appointments by phone, fax, or telex. Your counterparts in Singapore are quick to do business but big deals will likely require more than one trip.

It is not the intent of this book to provide legal or accounting advice. For these please consult a professional. Regulations are constantly changing and may be subject to arbitrary application. Use the information in this publication as a starting point and general guide. More detailed and current information may be obtained by consulting the services listed in Chapters Nine and Thirteen.

Establishing a Business in Singapore

Nearly a thousand American companies are currently doing business in Singapore. Finance companies are required to apply for special licenses. Such licenses are also required for the production of beer, firecrackers, pig iron, sponge iron, steel ingots, rolled and drawn steel products, refrigerators, air conditioners, cigarettes, cigars, and matches. Special societies and boards test and license professional practices. Once approval has been granted by the appropriate governing body a new company must register with the Registrar of Business or Registrar of Companies. Foreign companies should employ a local attorney for this purpose.

Investment and Tax Incentives

There are no restrictions on import of capital, remission of profits, and repatriation of original investment capital. Export expansion programs currently include double tax deductions for trade fairs and missions, overseas trade offices, overseas market development and similar activities. Market development assistance programs provide financial help to small export companies. These programs are administered by the Trade Development Board. The Pioneer Corporation and Export Expansion Corporation furnish tax incentives for new investment in key industries designated by the Economic Development Board. Currently the tax rate for locally incorporated companies and branch offices is thirty-three per cent. A variety of special deductions is available.

Business Law and Organization

The legal environment in Singapore is British in origin and nature. The operation of a business comes under the

Companies Act which is based on British law. Forms of business include private limited (incorporated) companies, sole proprietorships, partnerships, foreign company branch offices and representative offices. Local attorneys should be consulted when forming businesses because there is considerable paperwork involved.

At least one of the directors of an incorporated company must be a resident of Singapore. The branch office of a foreign company must have a registered office which must be open to the public for not less than five hours daily between nine a.m. and five p.m. Monday through Friday. Representative offices are not allowed to engage in trading activities. They can only serve as liaison or public relations offices. Any person entering Singapore to engage in business must apply for an employment pass from the Controller of Immigration. Dependents must apply for dependent passes.

Business Management

Societies build business cultures which reflect their dominant values. In this sense business is a social science. Management skills which are appropriate in one culture are not necessarily appropriate in another. There is a need among international managers for a deeper understanding of culturally determined value systems which should be considered when shifting management techniques from one nation to another. The range and scope of management activities are constrained by cultural considerations. One cannot successfully manage people without considering their culture, values, and beliefs.

The practice of nepotism is but one example. Most Western businesses have rules against it. But in Asian societies the worlds of work and family are not so easily separated. When you have a job opening your employees will suggest you hire their relatives. Employing many members of a family tends to merge family and company loyalties. This is a desirable objective in Asian business. Family owned corporations will place many relatives in management. Here loyalty will take precedence over competence.

Handling Employees

The mental and behavioral patterns of your employees were programmed long before they entered the business world. In your daily relationships with Chinese, Indian, and Malayan workers things which may seem small may have great cultural significance. Ask your assistant or secretary to help you over the immediate hurdles while you take the time to learn the culture in depth.

In collectivist societies such as Asia's the relationship between employer and employees involves distinct moral components which spring from the culture. There are complex intertwining obligations which reflect traditional values of the Asian family system. The employer is often expected to protect the employee, even one who is performing poorly. An employee is expected to display loyalty by never seeking other employment. He must try to perform adequately so his manager will not lose face. Most Westerners would consider this system to be too paternalistic.

Workers in Singapore expect to be viewed as whole persons, not as "hired hands." The best managers integrate the essence of the Asian kinship system into their corporate culture. They do not reward employees with huge bonuses which single out and separate individuals. Instead financial rewards may go to the group. Individuals are motivated with dignified personal gestures which convey trust and affection. In admonishing an employee a good manager must carefully consider an Asian's need for face and close personal relationships. All is family.

Over cocktails several American managers discussed their mishaps in handling employees. One, a plant manager of an industrial equipment company said his company had sent him to Singapore to replace a local manager who had been incurring heavy losses. To remedy this problem he sold assets, mostly inventory (to reduce liabilities and clean up the balance sheet), cut unprofitable lines of products, and fired forty-nine workers. In response to this "brutal efficiency" many of his employees resigned, he had problems hiring replacements, and production slowed. He now understood that his actions had been too hasty for the culture and should have involved persuasion and consultation. Another American manager had given his petite secretary a huge friendly bear hug to congratulate her for completing an assignment early. In shock and horror she quit!

Cultural differences can be convenient scapegoats for managerial shortcomings. An American project manager complained to me because he was behind schedule and had a progress report due in a few days. He blamed everything Singaporean: government bureaucracy, Indian workers, and Chinese supervisors. After more drinks and conversation it became evident that he alone was to blame. He had quantified everything to the last iota and had compulsively tabulated all the precise trivia of project management. But his schedule was foolishly unrealistic because it failed to account for local culture, equipment, and procedures.

Visiting Homes

If you are invited to visit the home of a customer, colleague, or employee consider it an honor. When visiting a Singaporean home remove your shoes if the family does. Sit only where and when you are asked. Seek out the older members of the family first to pay your respects. A small gift of cakes, candies, or fruits would be appreciated. Gifts in even numbers will bring good luck to a Chinese host. Gifts of money in even numbers produce bad luck for Malays. Flowers, clocks, sharp objects, and handkerchiefs have negative connotations for Chinese. To avoid embarrassing you your gift will not be opened in your presence.

For stays longer than a day gifts for a Malay host might include a cotton shirt. A Malay hostess would appreciate an

Indonesian *batik* in bright colors. Malay children like toys. But never give a toy dog. If you are entertaining Moslems keep your dog out of sight. Present your gifts at the end of the visit.

At dinner the host and hostess usually sit opposite each other. The wife of the host usually sits next to the wife of the guest. Do not sit at the table or start to eat until invited by the host. In a Chinese home the table setting may include chopsticks, forks, and spoons. There will be no knives because they are considered weapons. The food will be prepared in bite sizes. In an Indian or Malay home food is usually eaten with the fingers of the right hand, not the palm. As a guest never refuse food or drink. Always eat a nibble even when not hungry. It may be considered polite to leave a small amount of food on your plate to show there was enough to eat. Guests usually do not visit the bathroom without asking the host. A Singaporean hostess usually leads the ladies to the bathroom soon after dinner. When you leave a Malay home never say "goodby." Just say "I'll leave and come back."

Symbolic and Non-Verbal Communication

To be successful you will need a keen awareness of symbolic and non-verbal meanings. As a Westerner you may have to overcome the stereotype of a hairy, meat-smelling giant who speaks in a booming voice and phones Moslems between six-thirty and seven-thirty, the time for evening prayers.

The areas of non-verbal and symbolic communications are fraught with pitfalls because Asians are more subtle than Westerners. For example, our emphatic gesture of hitting a fist against the open palm of the opposite hand has obscene connotations in Singapore. It is rude to point or beckon at another person with your finger. Instead beckon with your whole hand, palm down. Never touch another person's head, particularly a child's. Try to avoid exposing the soles of your shoes or feet. Do not cross your legs in the presence of elders.

Colors have distinct meanings which must be considered when sending invitations, decorating dinner tables, and wrapping gifts. You would not want these done in black, the American funeral color. For many Asians, particularly Chinese, not only black, but white and blue signify death. Red, pink, and yellow evoke joy.

Odd numbers have negative meanings for Chinese. Four is pronounced with a sound similar to the word for death. Seven is unlucky. Even birds are symbolic; the stork connotes maternal death.

.

8. Bargaining

Patterns of Thought

In Singapore you may find yourself negotiating with visiting Asians as well as Singaporeans. This increases the importance of understanding Asian thought processes.

For Westerners the primary pattern of thought is linear. Series of logical relationships, such as cause and effect, extend in one direction. For Asians, webs of intuitive relationships create intricate, reciprocal patterns which extend in many directions. Asians place greater importance on fixed relationships. They will modify facts to make them conform to established thought patterns. In contrast Westerners will usually adjust patterns to fit the facts. This reality can work to your advantage if you take the time to understand the patterns which govern your counterpart's thought and behavior. For example, your primary goal may be to buy at the lowest price. Your Singaporean counterpart may be willing to meet your price but might be concerned about how a deal with you might disrupt an intricate long-standing relationship with his current distributor. You will not succeed unless you recognize and resolve this concern. To do so you must offer alternatives which meet your linear goals without tearing your counterpart's web. You might do this by structuring your offer so it will benefit you, your counterpart, *and* his current distributor. Your goal should be to enter the web by building long-term relationships in which everyone benefits.

Protocol

Singapore's business environment is probably the most modern in Asia. But some important aspects of traditional Chinese, Malay, and Indian cultures must still be considered. During introductions older people should be mentioned by name first. Always ask about a person's family. Treat business cards with great respect. Present them by holding the corners so your name can be read by the recipient. Do not fold, tear, or spindle a business card. Do not nonchalantly toss it into a bowl or pocket. Here a person's name is treated with great respect.

Names of Asians are often confusing to Westerners. Many Chinese give their family names first, followed by their generation and given name. This is the traditional order. But more modern Chinese might give their names in Western order. Many Indians do not have surnames. They simply place the first initial of their father's given name before their own. The "H" in H. Ramathan stands for the first letter of Ramathan's father's given name. Sikhs and Malays use "son of" in a fashion described in an earlier chapter.

Rules for introductions involving women are as varied as Singapore's cultures. Among Chinese a man shakes a woman's hand only if she offers it. Among Malays and Indians people of different sexes usually do not shake hands. Indian women may respond to introductions with the traditional palms together prayer-like greeting or just a nod and smile.

Entertaining

Asians do not let strangers into their webs. Socializing allows both sides to get the feel of the situation before discussing specifics. This will probably involve entertaining your counterpart.

Invitations must be clearly offered and confirmed. Indians particularly seem to have a penchant for misunderstanding invitations. Be sure to specify the date, time, place, and individuals invited. Do not ask a Moslem to eat during the fast of Ramadan.

If you are responsible for organizing a multi-ethnic dinner, you will have some problems planning the menu. Moslem Malays and Indians do not eat pork. Hindus do not eat beef. Many Indians are vegetarians. For this reason multi-ethnic meals are easier to hold at restaurants than at home. You will usually be entertained at a private club and may reciprocate at such prestigious restaurants as the Gordon Grill in the Westin Plaza or the Inn of Happiness at the Hilton.

Women usually order through the host. It is customary to discuss business during meals but one should wait until a beverage and the first course are served. Business is not discussed if wives are present.

At a Chinese meal never rest chopsticks on the dinner plate or rice bowl. Chopsticks are never inserted upright in rice except at funerals. Rest the narrow ends of chopsticks on a rest stand or soy sauce dish and the wide ends on the table. Avoid pointing chopsticks at another person. The soup spoon should be dipped toward you, not away. For Chinese toasts hold the glass in your left hand and rest its bottom on the open fingers of your right hand. Moslems eat with the fingers of the right hand. They consider the left hand, which is reserved for cleaning oneself with water after defecation, as unclean. Do not use your left hand for eating, handshakes, or exchanging objects when with Moslems.

Unlike the Chinese, Indians often linger for conversation after dinner. If you are the host pay the bill in advance to avoid arguments over who will pay. Men usually do not expect women to pay for meals.

Bargaining

If you have read the other books in *The Global Business Series* you know that the bargaining process with Asians is usually subtle, devious, and prolonged. In comparison nego-

tiations in Singapore are quicker and more direct. But you still
need to pay attention to basics. Be sure you are dealing with
a decision maker. Determine your "walk away" point early
and stick to it. Understand your counterpart's goals. Stress
common ground and areas of agreement rather than problems and differences. Prepare a list of concessions you can
offer the other side without hurting yours. Do not be surprised if your counterpart begins by discussing the possibility
of buying your product at a high price. His employer may
compensate him on the "discount" he obtains from the "initial
price." Arrive before your announced date and keep the date
of your departure secret so the other side cannot keep you
too busy to contact their competition. Singaporean business
people are tough negotiators, particularly on prices and dead-
lines. But you will find such a variety of possibilities for deals
that they will challenge your imagination. Stay open, loose,
and creative and your firm will benefit.

In Singapore friends, relatives, and established business
acquaintances get better deals than strangers. Loyalty is more
important than fairness. This is difficult for Westerners to
understand and accept. For Westerners business tasks take
priority over relationships; for Asians relationships are more
important than tasks. You will need to continue building a
personal relationship even after bargaining has started. In
addition to hosting meals this could involve thoughtful gifts,
rendering services, and sharing experiences. Some Americans
"break the ice" by taking their Singaporean to a *karaoke* bar
where patrons sing popular songs to taped accompaniment.

When dealing with Chinese a knowledge of Mandarin can
be helpful. Spoken Mandarin is no more difficult to learn than
a European language. An excellent school for short courses is
Pacific International Language School in Hawaii which offers a
new term every month. Some companies send executives
bound for Asia to Hawaii for language preparation.

The cultural problem most mentioned by American
executives was the difficulty in finding out what was actually

happening in the bargaining process. Asians are still inscrutable to Westerners. Enigmas result from the Asian preference for social harmony rather than openess. You will have to have all your cultural antennae fully extended to pick up the signals.

Many older Asians still do not want to lose face by saying *"no."* An officer of an American electronics firm showed me a letter he had received from a senior Asian executive in response to a business offer. It read something like this: "We received your proposal with great enthusiasm. It has been many years since our entire staff has been so excited by such a great idea. Your offer would produce great profit for us. We want to do business with you. Our chairman expressed his preference for a proposal from an old friend. But our joy at your offer is not diminished and we will always have warm memories regarding your firm." The American recipient of this letter said it took him several readings before he realized it was a rejection. He never understood the real reason his offer failed. In this case the use of an intermediary third party might have uncovered weaknesses in the competing proposal which might have been exploited without causing anyone to lose face.

To save face some Asians may continue to negotiate long after they have closed a deal with your competition. They are simply too embarrassed to say "no." By their values it is better to waste your time in fruitless bargaining. This is more likely to happen with Asians from other nations visiting Singapore than with Singaporean business people.

Bribery

In many regions of the world businesses routinely pay bribes to secure contracts, increase or maintain business, or avoid red tape. But not in Singapore. Here the government is scrupulously honest. Do nothing that even suggests bribery. Such an offer could subject you to strokes of the cane in

Singapore and even more painful fines and prison terms (under the 1977 Foreign Corrupt Practices Act) when you return to the United States.

Do not give government officials any presents. You can honor a business counterpart by presenting inexpensive gifts, such as flowers, candy, or pens with your company logo. These are especially innocuous if they may be shared by everyone in your counterpart's office. There may be legal, indirect ways to favor your counterpart, such as helping his son enroll in an American college. Before considering this type of inducement you should confer with your corporate attorney.

Counter Trade

Business people in Singapore are reluctant to talk about their counter trade activities. Although such trade is certainly legal it requires much imagination. Managers who learn to structure counter trade transactions acquire immense advantages over their competition. It is no wonder they treat their techniques as proprietary property!

Counter trade may involve barter, a straight swap of goods or services; counter purchase, in which goods may be brought for resale to a third party to get foreign exchange for payment; offsets, involving payments to a nation to make up for its loss of income, production, or jobs; or buy back compensation, in which an investment in mining or manufacturing is repaid with minerals or processed goods produced by the investment. Counter trade can produce substantial profits for one who can use imagination and has enough persistence to clear away the intricate screens of bureaucratic underbrush.

An American executive said a deal he had closed with a third world company had been blocked because the customer's nation had no hard currency. Since the customer could not pay in cash it offered shoes in payment for the American's machine tools. When the American informed his boss about this proposal he was almost laughed out of the office: "loafers or casuals?" After frequent painful increases in the value of the dollar the American company became desperate for sales. The executive contacted a commodity broker in Singapore who arranged to sell the shoes for more than the list price of the machine tools. The deal was closed and resulted in nearly seven hundred thousand dollars in sales for the American company. Since this first exposure to the wonderful world of counter trade this executive has made a fortune for his company in similar deals. Some of his recent transactions involved as many as five products and four nations: tuna for cameras for tools; computers for scrap metal for tools; coffee for cars for tools. In 1985 his machine tool company set up a counter trade subsidiary which now does more business than the parent company.

Counter trade has long been favored by communist nations which are chronically short of hard currency. Although accurate estimates are not available somewhere between twelve and twenty-six per cent of world trade appears to be counter trade. International organizations such as the Organization of Petroleum Exporting Companies, the International Monetary Fund, and the International Coffee Organization often disapprove of counter trade because it can be used to violate pricing and export agreements. Individual nations such as the United States sometimes oppose counter trade because it makes price evaluations for tariffs difficult and complicates the compilation of statistical trade data.

Yet the infinity of possible combinations boggles the mind. In recent counter trade deals Honduras exchanged bananas for Russian fertilizer, Libya supplied Uganda with oil for coffee, Saudi Arabia traded oil for British war planes, and Germany exchanged trucks with Mongolia for the bones of a dinosaur!

In recent years American laws have begun to encourage some kinds of barter by waiving some provisions of antitrust regulations. Singapore is a natural venue for counter trade activities because of its excellent communications and trading expertise. Singapore also offers special tax incentives for counter trade.

Getting Paid

Your bargaining should always include means and time of payment. There are five basic methods of payment, ranked from the most to the least secure: cash in advance, letter of credit, documentary drafts for collection, open account, and consignment sales. For new exporters or exporters selling to new markets, letters of credit arranged through major international banks offer a safe and expedient way of doing business abroad.

9. How to Get Help

Sources of Assistance

The United States exports only about nine per cent of its gross national product compared to roughly twenty-seven percent for most other industrial nations. Few small and medium-sized American business export. Many seem reluctant to ask for help from our government. Perhaps they fear red tape. The bureaucratic maze is indeed confusing. Yet the help provided by the United States government is expert, timely, effective and often free. There is also a wide variety of assistance available from agencies of the government of Singapore and business and private organizations in both nations. Of the nearly one thousand American firms operating in Singapore most had some outside help in starting. You need only ask what help is available. Singapore's Capital Assistance Scheme, for example, provides financial assistance to companies developing projects of special benefit to the island. The Economic Development Board can provide up to half the necessary equity with a sell back provision. In addition, loans, payable in one to ten years, can be made available for up to eighty-five per cent of fixed assets.

Addresses are listed in Chapter Thirteen.

ASSISTANCE FROM THE
GOVERNMENT OF SINGAPORE

Type of Help	*Agency*
Obtaining entry and employment passes	The Controller, Immigration
Establishing a business	The First Secretary (Commercial) Singapore Embassy, Washington, D.C. and regional offices of Singapore Economic Development Board in New York, Los Angeles, Houston, Santa Clara (CA), New Canaan (CT), and Chicago
Information on trade and shipping investments . . .	Trade and Shipping Investment Division, Ministry of Trade and Industry
Arranging Finance, Foreign Exchange, Insurance	Managing Director, Monetary Authority
Registration of company	The Registrar, Registration of Companies
Registration of business names	The Registrar, Registration of Businesses
Obtaining trade marks and patents	The Registrar, Registry of Trade Marks and Patents
Obtaining factory space and industrial land	Director, Land and Estates Division, Jurong Town Corporation or Chief, Estates and Land Office, Housing and Development Board
Arranging Land Surveys	The Secretary, Land Surveys Board

ASSISTANCE FROM BUSINESSES AND PRIVATE ORGANIZATIONS IN SINGAPORE

Type of Help	*Organization(s)*
Obtaining Legal Assistance	The Secretary, Law Society of Singapore
Obtaining Engineering Services	The Registrar, Professional Engineers Board
Obtaining Hotel License	The Secretary, Hotel Licensing Board
Relocation to Singapore	Relocation Services, such as Orientations
Locating Accounting Services	Singapore Society of Accountants
Locating Architectural Services	Singapore Board of Architects
Investment Briefings	The American Business Council

ASSISTANCE FROM THE U.S. GOVERNMENT

The Department of Agriculture

The Department of Agriculture maintains domestic and overseas offices which help American businesses establish foreign contacts. It also provides help in locating over-seas buyers and offers a direct mail service to American food exporters.

The Department of Commerce

The Foreign Commercial Service of the U.S. Department of Commerce has an office at the U.S. Embassy in Singapore. Upon request it will send pamphlets such as *Foreign Eco-*

nomic Trends, American Investments in Singapore, and *How to Set Up a Business in Singapore.*

The Department of Commerce sponsors trade and investment missions. Its *Market Share Reports* identify overseas markets. *World Data Reports,* published by Commerce, provides credit information on foreign firms. The Office of Major Contracts assists American businesses in obtaining large foreign contracts.

The International Trade Administration, an agency of the Department of Commerce, is organized into trade development sections in such industry sectors as capital goods, consumer goods, transportation, and industrial goods and services. Its staff includes experts on every country in the world including communist nations. The International Trade Administration offers assistance ranging from export mailing lists to product marketing services.

Through its Foreign Commercial Service and other arms, Commerce can locate qualified local representatives, evaluate local firms, and help with marketing programs. It helps with market research, trade fairs, and even closing sales. The Foreign Commercial Service has helped thousands of American businesses close their first overseas sales. Your first step is to contact the nearest district office of the Department of Commerce.

The Export-Import Bank

According to the Export-Import Bank some eighteen thousand small American businesses are missing sales opportunities abroad. The Export-Import Bank develops America's export potential by encouraging small and medium-sized businesses to export goods and services. It offers an array of loans, guarantees, and insurance programs. The Foreign Credit Insurance Corporation acts as an agent for the Export-Import Bank to insure American exporters against non-payment by foreign buyers.

The Small Business Administration

The Small Business Administration guarantees export financing and is geared to meet the needs of small businesses entering export markets for the first time. The Small Business Administration publishes *Exporter's Guide to Federal Resources for Small Business*. This guide supplies names, addresses and phone numbers of contacts in each agency who can provide help to small businesses. It is available for only $3.50 from the Superintendent of Documents.

The State Department

The State Department's Office of Business and Export Affairs publishes information on the important topic of political risk for American businesses considering or conducting foreign operations.

Local Agencies

Many state, county, and municipal agencies have programs to help American firms develop overseas business.

ASSISTANCE FROM BUSINESSES AND ORGANIZATIONS IN THE U.S.

Credit Specialists

Credit companies, such as Dun and Bradstreet, can provide financial evaluations on thousands of foreign firms.

U.S. Attorneys Specializing in Foreign Law

A list of attorneys who specialize in foreign law may be obtained from the International Trade Administration, Department of Commerce.

Training Courses

American University in Washington, D.C. sponsors an excellent program to prepare American executives for overseas assignments. Thunderbird School in Arizona has longer programs. One of the best schools for short courses in Mandarin is Pacific Language School in Honolulu which has been training executives in this Chinese language since 1979.

Trading Companies

A 1982 law allowing the formation of trading companies benefits both small and medium-sized companies wishing to trade abroad. Firms can now join together to form export trading companies.

Some of the provisions of U.S. antitrust laws are now nullified for purposes of trading companies. The International Trade Administration will provide information on ways that firms can obtain protection from federal and state antitrust laws and will provide assistance in locating other firms interested in forming trading companies.

BankAmerica World Trade Corporation is an example of a trading company formed to meet the challenge of foreign competition. It offers a full range of services which include export, import, third country and counter trade transactions. This company will take title to goods and act as a broker or joint business partner. Other services relate to international transportation, insurance, and finance. A staff of area and product specialists provides expertise for international transactions.

PART THREE

Singapore:
The Personal Experience

This handbook is not intended to be a tourist guide but I am including information which should increase your enjoyment of Singapore.

There will be considerable overlap between your personal and business activities. Your adjustment to Singapore and your understanding of its people will enhance your business effectiveness.

The more you enjoy Singapore and its people the greater success you will have in your business endeavors.

10. Travel Tips

Passports and Visas

Seasoned international business travelers avoid delaying trips by keeping passports, visas, and inoculations current. A United States passport is required for Americans to enter Singapore. Americans visiting as tourists or for social purposes do not need a Singapore visa. The visitor must be in possession of onward or return tickets and ample funds. The period of stay allowed is normally two weeks but it can be easily extended by application to the Controller of Immigration. Visas are required for visitors on business.

Timing the Visit

Singapore is always warm and humid. The daily average high temperature is eighty-seven degrees. The average daily low is seventy-five degrees. The temperature seldom exceeds ninety-five degrees because sea breezes preclude higher temperatures. The city gets about one hundred inches of rain a year compared to about thirty inches for Chicago. Rainfall tends to be heaviest between November and January due to the northeast monsoon. Some business people prefer to visit in July, the driest month. It is best not to visit during the Chinese New Year since little business is done at this time and hotels are full.

Health Precautions

Singapore requires inoculations for yellow fever, typhoid, and cholera only for people arriving from areas infected with these diseases.

Some Westerners prefer to obtain vaccinations for hepatitis. It is always a good idea to keep basic vaccinations, such as tetanus, cholera, typhoid, polio, and yellow fever current. Some of these are required for entry to other nations in south and southeast Asia. Since some vaccinations take time for full effect you should plan early.

Packing

Most business offices in Singapore are air conditioned so suits are standard wear. First class restaurants usually require a jacket and tie. Clothes of natural fibers are more comfortable than synthetics in Singapore's high humidity. By packing some small items you can avoid wasting time on shopping trips. These items might include gift wrap paper for items purchased en route, small sewing and first aid kits, toilet paper (planes have been known to run out), extra eyeglasses, dental floss, cold remedies, and folding hangers for steaming clothing wrinkles above a bathtub.

Departure from the United States

It is best not to exchange large amounts of American money into Singapore dollars at your departure point in the United States. The exchange rate is usually less favorable at airport money exchanges than at hotels and banks in Singapore. Many business travelers take small amounts of Singapore currency for initial expenses. Traveler's checks in small denominations can be helpful. Major credit cards are honored almost everywhere and can be used as identity to cash checks at most hotels. Major credit card companies charge lower currency exchange conversion fees than banks and hotels. Some business people delay exchanging money when the dollar is rising by carrying traveler's checks in American dollars. When the dollar is falling they try to prepay bills and obtain prices guaranteed in American currency.

The duty-free shop at the departure airport is a good place to buy gifts for business associates in Singapore.

If you are carrying expensive foreign manufactured items when leaving the United States you an avoid paying customs duties upon your return by registering them before departure.

En Route

Your trans-Pacific flight to Singapore will take at least twelve hours, considerably more if you change planes en route. Most non-direct trips take between twenty-two and twenty-seven hours including airport stops. As you fly west-ward you will gain an hour as you cross each time zone but will lose a full day at the International Date Line. This is enough to disorient anyone.

You can reduce the effects of jet lag by restricting your consumption of food and alcohol, sleeping at least six hours on the plane, and taking several walks during the flight.

Arrival in Singapore

Customs at Changi Airport is polite and efficient. There is no restriction on the amount of local and foreign currency which may be carried in or out of the country. Duty-free articles include two hundred cigarettes or fifty cigars or two hundred and fifty grams of tobacco, one quart of wine, beer, or spirits, and business samples of no commercial value.

The taxi fare from the airport to downtown costs about ten American dollars. A bus, available from the lower level of the airport, costs fifty cents.

When you arrive in Singapore your body's circadian rhythm will still be set on American time. Singapore is eleven hours ahead of New York. Noon in Singapore is one A.M. in New York and ten P.M. the previous day in Los Angeles, standard time.

If you arrive in Singapore in the morning you can alleviate jet lag by taking a short nap as soon as you reach the hotel. Then enjoy a light lunch. If you arrive in the evening resist the need to sleep until your normal bed time.

Minimizing Costs

In Asia Americans have a reputation for overly generous tipping. There is generally no tipping in Singapore. In hotels and restaurants service charges of ten per cent and taxes of three per cent are added to your bill. If you tip fifteen per cent these costs will add thirty-three per cent to your bill!

Hotel rates vary considerably. Most business hotels will range in cost from sixty to one hundred and fifty American dollars per day. This is considerably less than equivalent rooms in Hong Kong or Tokyo. Some hotels add huge surcharges on long distance telephone calls. These charges can more than double the costs. You can avoid these by using AT&T's USADirect which bypasses local phone systems. Use of a telephone credit card can also save money. A list of business hotels is included in Chapter Thirteen.

Getting Around in Singapore

It is best not to drive in Singapore. It takes a while to get used to driving on the left side of the road by using a steering wheel on the right side of the car. There is a very complicated system of licenses, stickers, and hours for access to the special downtown traffic area.

For short business trips it may be better to use convenient and reasonably priced taxis. Cabbies speak English. Few rides within the city cost more than five American dollars. There is no bargaining for price. The cabbie should start the meter at the beginning of the trip. There are additional charges for extra people, air conditioning, and luggage. You need not tip cabbies.

A few words of Malay can make a good impression. *Silakin,* "Please," and *terima kasih,* "Thank you" have the same value everywhere. So do *permisi,* "Excuse me" and *ma 'af,* "Sorry."

Health Precautions

Singapore is one of few places in Asia which produces tap water fit to drink. Health and sanitary standards are high. Most problems are likely to arise, not from visits to Singapore, but from side trips to such exotic places as Bali, Bhutan, or Burma. Even nearby Malaya, Indonesia, and Thailand have serious biohazards. These countries are worth visiting but you should have health insurance which includes medical evacuation. Your "little black bag" could include anti-fever, anti-pain, anti-nausea, and anti-diarrhea medicines, band-aids, antibiotics, suntan and sunburn lotions, antihistamines, water purifiers, insect repellent, cough syrup, and chloroquine or pyramethaminesulfadoxine for malaria. Some of these require a doctor's prescription.

You can reduce the need for medicines by avoiding milk products and uncooked vegetables. Eat only meat and sea-food which have been thoroughly cooked and are still hot. Tea and Chinese food just off the wok should be safe. So are bottled water, beer, and soft drinks. Avoid ice. Always wear shoes and keep covered against mosquitoes.

There are no sure precautions. In 1967 I came down with a bad case of salmonella in Bandung, Indonesia, and was taken to a missionary hospital where I received the last rites of a faith not mine. It took three months to recover. Adventure requires risks!

Departure and Return to the United States

There is a six dollar departure tax in Singapore. On the flight back to the United States you will gain a day at the

International Date Line but lose an hour crossing each time zone. United States Customs allows you to bring back four hundred dollars worth of purchases duty free. If you stay outside the United States thirty-one days or more this goes up. If you exceed the limit you will have to pay a ten per cent duty on the first six hundred dollars over the four hundred dollars exemption. At this point it gets more complicated. It is best to check with customs first if you plan large purchases. It is a good idea to pack your purchases in a separate suitcase to avoid delay at customs. They are usually understanding about product samples.

11. Living in Singapore

Moving

Moving to Singapore is much different than moving to another part of the United States. You can make your move to Singapore much easier by hiring a relocation service (such as Transition Support Services) and purchasing a copy of *Living in Singapore* from the American Association of Singapore. Both of these organizations have expertise concerning expatriate life and problems. A relocation service can sometimes pay for itself by reducing temporary hotel stays, negotiating prices for housing and servants, and registering children in schools.

Preparation for the move, including passports, visas, inoculations, and shipping of household goods should begin about six months in advance. You may wish to bring along special items which may be difficult to find or unavailable in Singapore. These might include your favorite books, pens and cartridges, cosmetics, toiletries, spices, and cooking utensils. Bring extra eyeglasses, contact lens, and prescription medicines. Although Singapore exports much clothing in Western sizes these may be difficult to find on the island. American holiday items such as artificial Christmas trees and children's Halloween costumes may be hard to find. Do not pack anything you will need during your trip or while waiting for your goods (which will take one or two months in transit). Save some time to check your insurance for overseas coverage, cancel your utilities, obtain an international driver's license, and grant someone a power of attorney for business or personal matters.

Arrival

Singapore requires foreigners to acquire employment and dependent passes. Applications should be made prior to arrival since approval could take some months. Companies usually obtain these passes for their employees. Permits are issued for one to five years and may be renewed. There are a variety of programs through which foreign investors can acquire permanent residence.

Duties are not levied on personal effects or household goods imported in reasonable quantities. To obtain your shipped goods you will have to present your passport and work pass when you claim them. Some items such as fireworks, pornography, weapons, and certain types of radio equipment may not be imported. Your video tapes will be confiscated and sent to the Board of Censors for viewing. You will be charged a censorship fee for this service. If you have videos needed for business sales presentations or employee training you should submit them for censorship well before they are needed.

There is no rabies in Singapore. Imported dogs must be licensed, inoculated, leashed, and quarantined for at least thirty days. Shots and licenses should be arranged in advance.

There are many hotels suitable to stay in while waiting for housing. They are in all price categories. Many offer babysitting services.

It is a good idea to register your name, address, and passport number at the U.S. Embassy. This will make it easier to obtain travel advisories and replace lost passports. You may also wish to make credit arrangements with a local hospital and physician.

Cultural Shock

Life can be difficult when familiar rules and signs are left behind. Anxiety can develop from not knowing what to expect. You will feel like an interloper in a strange society.

Cultural shock usually involves four phases. In the first you will be staying in a hotel and enjoying a virtual vacation on this exotic island. Everything will seem new and exciting. The second stage will involve the myriad frustrations of moving into a house, meeting people from another culture, and finding your way around. In the third stage cultural problems may seem overwhelming. Every contact with the alien culture may produce misery. Even going to a public toilet may be a problem. Most are squat types with no paper. What do you do with the bailing scoop and water? You may draw inward and refuse contact with anything not American thus pretending you are still in the United States. You may count the days and hours until your return. If you survive the third stage without becoming an ethnocentric hermit or escaping from the island you will enter the fourth phase. In it you will learn to accept the island's cultures on their own terms and enjoy the new experiences and perspectives they offer.

Singapore's unique variety of English English can create communication difficulties. "Out of station" means out of town. People "shift" houses rather than move, make "trunk" rather than long distance calls, and take a "lift" rather than an elevator from the "void deck." When your dinner guest says he will "make a move" it means he will go home. "Indented" merchandise is out of stock. A business with a hundred parking "lots" has space for only one hundred cars. Such language problems can add to cultural shock.

Singapore should not be too much of a shock to your bank account. Although most necessities, such as housing, food, and utilities will cost more than you may be used to paying in the United States, they will be considerably lower than prices in Tokyo or Taipei.

Much of your business success will depend upon your personal ability to adjust to life in Singapore. To be most effective for your firm you will need to break out of your thick Western cultural shell and learn to think and act in new ways. Then you will become your company's wise and valuable Singapore expert.

The American Community

According to a recent study there are about seven thousand American expatriates living in Singapore. They stay an average of three to four years. The center for this community is the American Association. It was founded in 1917 to provide educational facilities for children of American expatriates. Today it is the umbrella organization which includes all other American community organizations. It is involved in social and cultural activities such as the Fourth of July picnic, the Boy Scouts, and the Singapore American Cultural Fund.

Housing

Housing ranges from modest apartments to luxurious estates. Most of the housing is so new there are few neighborhoods as Americans know them. Black and White houses date to the colonial period and are leased by the government. They have all the romantic appeal and inconveniences of imperial life: high ceilings, overhead fans, bamboo "chick" blinds, white plaster walls with black wood trim, spacious gardens, inadequate storage, antiquated external electrical wiring, small bathrooms and kitchens, no water heaters or air conditioners. They are rented without furnishings or appliances.

Newer housing includes detached, duplex, and apartment buildings. Most have air conditioning. A room for a maid is fairly standard.

A wide variety of rental housing is available. Except for high rise condominiums non-citizens must obtain government approval to purchase housing.

Classified ads in the *Straits Times* and other papers list large selections of housing for sale and rent. Real estate agents are readily available. The act of viewing property for rental or purchase is itself a cultural shock. Many houses and apartments are in poor states of repair. Singaporeans do not prepare houses or apartments to make them attractive for sale or rental. Leases run for one or two years. You can require an escape clause in case your company moves you out of town. You will be required to make a deposit of one to three months rent and pay a government stamp duty tax. Electricity is 220/240 volts, 50 cycle alternating current. American appliances require transformers which are sold in Singapore. American television sets will not work on the island. Radios and stereos will do fine with transformers. Rental and second hand electrical appliances are easily available.

Automobiles

When you arrive in Singapore you can use your American driver's license for fourteen days or an International Driver's License valid for three months. Beyond that you must obtain a Singapore driver's license at the traffic police office on Maxwell Road. You will need to present a valid driver's license, a passport, and pay a fee. Your Singapore license will be good for one to three years depending upon the amount paid. It can be renewed at your local post office. It is a good idea to buy a highway code book to study Singapore's rules of the road.

It can take a while to get used to driving on the left side of the road by using a steering wheel on the right side of the car. Signals in Singapore can be confusing to strangers. A hand appearing from the driver's (right) side means right turn if it is waving in a counter-clockwise circle and left turn if it is not moving. A branch of a shrub inserted into a bumper or rear mudguard indicates the car is out of order.

There are complicated procedures for buying, registering, and licensing new cars. Heavy taxes and fees are imposed in order to limit the numbers of vehicles on the roads. You must provide proof of insurance to register your vehicle. If you use your vehicle to teach someone to drive you must obtain learner's plates. If a vehicle displaying learner's plates is involved in an accident the driver is presumed by the law to be at fault.

Household Servants

There is a shortage of servants in Singapore. Some thirty thousand amahs (maids) from the Philippines work in Singapore. Many others come from Thailand and Sri Lanka. Most speak little English. As soon as they learn to speak English well they quit for better jobs. Probably the best way to obtain a household employee is from another Westerner who is leaving the island. Then you will likely have an employee who is honest, reliable, and used to a Western household. Private and government employment services are also available.

Since most Americans are not accustomed to having servants the experience can be difficult. If you like to putter around the kitchen your cook might consider it an invasion of her domain. Before hiring a servant clearly establish such details as dates for salary reviews, annual bonuses, health examinations, provision of quarters, furniture, bedding, and food for live-ins, and the amount of termination pay. Live-in amahs from abroad usually work on a two year contract. Some will cook and shop. Certain Moslem servants will not prepare pork or work in a house with a dog.

If your maid works more than fourteen hours per week you must contribute to the Central Provident Fund. On your servant's most important annual holiday you are expected to pay a bonus equal to one month's pay. This holiday is Hari Raya for Moslems, Deepavali for Indians, and the Asian New Year for Chinese. If your servant has worked for you less than a year a reasonable portion of one month's pay is due.

Singapore's supermarkets sell a great variety of foods. Most are imported and cost more than in the United States. If you have no servant to shop you can use a provisioner. This person, for a fee, will call you in the morning for your shopping list and deliver the food items in the afternoon.

Utilities

To apply for electricity, water, gas, and garbage collection you will need to visit the Public Utilities Board on

Somerset Road. You should bring your passport, a letter from your landlord stating your name and date of occupancy, and a cash deposit. The island's excellent telephone service is administered by Telecoms. To have a telephone installed obtain an application from any post office or call Telecoms about a week in advance. Telephones rent for about one hundred American dollars per month.

Postal Service

Mail is delivered daily Monday through Saturday. Singapore's postal system is fast and efficient. Locations of branch offices are listed in the front of the telephone directory. Parcels from abroad are held for Customs inspection. You will have to visit the Dutiable Parcels Station on Chai Chee Road or send someone with identification and authorization to retrieve these parcels.

Newspapers

English language newspapers in Singapore include *The Straits Times, The Business Times, The International Herald Tribune,* and *USA Today. The Financial Times* and *Times of London* are available in air mail editions. *The Singapore American* is written especially for American expatriates. It is loaded with practical advice and news of the American community.

Radio and Television

Sets must be licensed annually by owners and renters. Forms for this purpose are available at the post offices. Fees are required. Much of the programming is in English. The government censors sex and violence in broadcasting.

Health

The medical system in Singapore is different from the United States. Singapore doctors have an MBBS (bachelor of medicine) rather than an M.D. In the United States medical board certification is granted at the end of a training program while in Singapore the degree is granted first. The American medical payment system is based upon insurance; Singapore's is based on cash up front. Be prepared to pay a large cash deposit in advance when you visit a doctor or hospital. Credit cards and medical insurance are just beginning to be used. Under certain conditions you might be able to join Singapore's MediSave scheme. Most businesses establish credit relationships with hospitals for their employees. Singapore has many fine hospitals such as Mount Elizabeth Hospital, the American Hospital, and Jurong Hospital.

Singapore's health standards are excellent. But the high heat and humidity can wear one out over a period of time. Skin diseases, fungus infections, sunstroke and heat exhaustion are easy to contract. It makes sense to get sufficient sleep, avoid too much sun, drink plenty of water, and rinse fruits and vegetables. Children should wear shoes when playing outside to avoid parasites. Health hazards include jellyfish, sea urchins, stingrays, cobras, krafts, pit vipers, scorpions, and centipedes. Most will not attack unless surprised or threatened.

Children and Schools

Children often adjust more easily to expatriate life than adults. In Singapore your family will be closely knit. You will share many new experiences. Children who have lived abroad often develop a mature independence at an earlier age.

There is a wide variety of foreign schools in Singapore. Most American children attend schools based on the American educational system. The Singapore American School provides education from pre-kindergarten to the twelfth grade on two campuses. The International School covers the same grades plus the American community college level. The Far Eastern Academy is operated by the Seventh Day Adventist

Church primarily for mission children. There are other schools based upon British, French, German, Dutch, Japanese, Chinese, and Swiss educational systems. Many American firms pay all or part of school tuition for dependents.

Reverse Cultural Shock

When you return to the United States you will again experience cultural shock. This reverse shock can be quite difficult because there is likely to be substantial social change in the United States during your absence. American values, social movements, politics, habits, and speech are probably the most dynamic in the world. You can keep track of these changes by reading American news magazines and talking with newly arrived Americans.

Other problems upon your return may involve adjusting to life without servants and catching up on business changes.

12. Things To Do, See, and Learn

A New Perspective

Although this is not intended to be a tourist guidebook I am including things to do, see, and learn. Your ability to enjoy Singapore will have a direct impact upon your business efficiency. Your direct exposure to the many cultures of Singapore will give you new insights into your own. You will have immense opportunities for business and personal growth.

Part-time Tourism

Singapore is easy to explore because you can go anywhere in a few hours. Abundant information is available from the Singapore Tourist Promotion Board and travel agencies in the city. This is but a brief preview of the island's tourist attractions.

To tour Singapore is to enter a world of legend. You might start by ordering a Singapore sling at the Raffles Hotel and viewing the billiards room where guests once shot an intruding tiger. Then you might visit the Jurong Bird Park to have your fortune told by inscrutable feathered friends. The evening might feature a bumboat (motorized sampan) ride up the Singapore River.

Singapore is called the "Garden City" with good reason. Its botanical gardens established in 1859, present the world's finest collection of palms and orchids. The Chinese Garden, *Yu Hwa Yuan,* is designed to Sung Dynasty styles and specifications. Next to it is *Seiwaen,* the Japanese Garden, a place of great delicacy. The Singapore Zoo features Chinese red pandas (catbears), polar bears swimming for live fish, and tea parties with orangutans. Jurong Crocodile Paradise puts on a splashy crocodile wrestling show.

A visit to the Maritime Museum at Senrosa explains why the island has one of the world's busiest ports. The museum's Primitive Craft Gallery, Fisheries Gallery, and Fullerton Lighthouse vividly recall the role of the sea in shaping Singapore. Examples of the island's traditional handicrafts are displayed in the National Museum.

Singapore has a great diversity of cultural events: dragon dances for guest ghosts, festivals featuring fire walkers, processions of penitents with pierced tongues, and colorful kite-flying contests. Hardly a week goes by without a Chinese, Malay, Indian or Western cultural celebration. Between these events one can visit Chinatown (Boat Quay, Ann Siang Hill, Kreta Ayer Road), Little India (Serangoon Road) and Arab Street (Beach Road, Baghdad, Bussorah, Muscat, and Kandarah Streets). There are numerous Chinese, Hindu, and Buddhist temples, Moslem mosques, and Christian churches. Hindu temples are in the Dravidian style since most Indians are from south India. The oldest Christian church was founded by Armenians who arrived shortly after Raffles.

The island is uniquely situated for convenient side trips to neighboring nations. Malaya, Thailand, and Indonesia are close enough for weekend visits. A onc or two-week vacation allows sufficient time to visit any part of Asia.

Music and Drama

The Instant Cultural Show at the Cultural Theater on Grange Road performs a potpourri of music, dance, and Chinese opera. Here also the Singapore Experience presents a multi-screen audio-visual chronicle of Singapore's variegated past. The Raffles, Hyatt Regency, and Mandarin hotels also schedule cultural shows. The Victorian Theater in Empress

Place presents both Asian and Western drama, comedy, and ballet.

Some culture is free. During the Festival of Hungry Ghosts in late summer, *wayangs,* Chinese operas, are staged in the open air. The rest of the year one may attend *wayangs* every Saturday at the Singapore Handicraft Theater. Chinese operas are noisy spectacles but well worth seeing.

A variety of musical performances cater to every taste. The Singapore Symphony Orchestra sometimes plays Beethoven by an illuminated fountain. On Sunday mornings proud owners of singing birds bring their caged sopranos to the corner of Tiong Bahru and Seng Poh Roads to present an outdoor concert.

Sports

Singapore is a paradise for sports enthusiasts. One can play golf or tennis, horseback ride, canoe, sail, and water ski every day of the year. The island, although almost on the equator, sports an ice skating rink. There are opportunities to participate in bowling, cricket, tennis, racquetball, rugby, squash, and soccer. Many sports have organized teams for public play. Details of events can be obtained by checking the sports pages of newspapers or phoning the Singapore Sports Council.

The island's many resort areas also feature sports activities. Beautiful Batam is only twenty-five minutes from Singapore City by high speed ferry. It offers snorkeling, wind surfing, canoeing and scuba diving. The resort island of Sentosa offers facilities for pony and bicycle riding, golf, canoeing, sail board riding, and roller skating.

Singapore's sports clubs are world famous. The Singapore Cricket Club offers soccer, rugby, tennis, hockey, billiards, snooker, squash, and two restaurants as well as cricket. The Singapore Polo Club features polo, riding classes, tennis and squash courts, a swimming pool, a restaurant, care, and bar. Other fine clubs include the Singapore Tennis

Center, Jurong Country Club, Singapore Island Country Club, and Warren Golf Club. Membership in these clubs is not cheap. Your company might pay the fee if you can convince your boss membership will be a benefit for business. This will usually be true.

Shopping

The major participant sport in Singapore is shopping. Prices are often lower than elsewhere due to hot competition and the absence of import duties. Visitors shop till they drop, buy till they die, spend to the end.

The city bristles with stores. Almost every available space is committed to retail activity. A fine nutmeg orchard was torn out to build the huge shopping center on Orchard Road. New emporia rise to satisfy shopping euphoria.

Major items for sale include antiques, art objects, electronic and photographic equipment, watches, jewelry, crystal, porcelain, pewter, silks, perfumes, carpets, computers, cloisonne, sports equipment, and fashion wear. Bargains abound. But it is important to bargain for prices and delivery terms, obtain guarantees, and check the condition of the product.

Bargaining

In most large department stores and supermarkets prices are firmly fixed. Signs announce "no bargaining." In most smaller shops bargaining is standard. First obtain the asking price. Then offer half. As you come to terms on prices be sure you are paying less than you would in the United States. Do not make offers for more than you are willing to pay because you might be held to them. Always bargain with a smile and a sense of humor. It is part of the culture.

Goods purchased in Singapore may usually not be returned. Be sure to obtain international guarantees and warranties for cameras, watches, and appliances. For custom-made goods a deposit of half the purchase price is usually required. Traveler's checks and credit cards are normally accepted. But merchants might not ship goods until they have received payment from the credit card company. Be sure to get receipts for customs.

Most merchants are honest but a few swindlers cause problems. Be sure electrical appliances are working before you buy them. Check to ensure that accessories, such as camera cases, are packed with your purchase. "Associate Stores" post signs stating that they adhere to the high standards of the "Good Retailer Scheme." The government of Singapore will pay return travel expenses so a visitor who can prove he was cheated by a merchant can testify in court.

Dining

Singapore has such a variety of fine food that you will want to dine out often. Addresses of some excellent restaurants are listed in Chapter Thirteen.

Chinese cuisine includes food from every province: Cantonese spring rolls and steamed dumplings; Taiwanese stewed fish; Hunanese sweet-sour carp and steamed chicken; Peking duck, eel, and chicken; Shanghai braised shark fin; and Szechuan roast duck in camphor leaves. Culinary traditions originating in China's coastal provinces tend to be mild and colorful. Those from inland provinces such as Hunan and Szechuan are very hot. Singapore's delicious seafoods include salt and pepper prawns, crisp baby squid, and steamed sea bass.

Indian foods are primarily curries. Curries from south India are aromatic and fiercely hot creating incandescent tongues. Northern Indian curries are slightly milder, more subtle blends with almonds or yogurt. Prawn masala, banana leaf curry and *tandoori* chicken are favorite Indian dishes. *Mee goreng,* consisting of thick egg noodles fried with eggs, beancurd, and peas, is a favorite. Much of India's cuisine was influenced by Moghul invaders from the north who were relatives of the Mongols who influenced northern Chinese cooking. Both specialized in marinated, skewered meat, the inspiration for Indian *tandoori.* They also brought the habit of cooking with yogurt.

Malay cooking includes dishes originating in Indonesia. It is often highly spiced with tumeric and coriander. The most popular Malay food with visitors is *satay,* skewers of meat or poultry which are barbecued over charcoal and dipped in a sauce of sweet peanuts and coconut milk.

Many of these dishes will give you a new insight into the essence of water!

Most restaurants in major hotels feature standard American fare. Others offer Japanese, Korean, Thai, Vietnamese, Scandinavian, Swiss, Italian, French, and Mexican cuisine.

"Chilli" crabs may be Singapore's most popular dish. But every month produces a new culinary fad. There was a recent craze for drunken prawns, live prawns immersed in brandy before being cooked alive. This practice led to a flood of protest from animal rights and prohibition advocates.

Singapore's streets used to be cluttered with the carts of food hawkers. Some years ago the government moved them into large modern food centers where they are regularly checked for sanitation and health standards. A great variety of local foods can be enjoyed at low prices at such hawker centers as Newton Circus, People's Park, and Satay Club.

A person writing of Singapore's foods would be remiss by not mentioning its delightful array of exotic fruits: the yellow-green starfruit, named for its shape; the bright orange papaya, reputed to be a contraceptive when consumed by women; the orange-yellow nangka (jackfruit), the size of a watermelon, tasting like chestnuts; the egg shaped chiku, so musty in flavor; the duku, redolent of grapefruit; the spiny red rambutan, a cousin of the lychee; the sweet mangosteen, black skin concealing a delight of pure white pulp; and the malodorous but tasty durian, the only fruit a tiger craves.

Night Life

Singapore's somewhat sedate night life centers on hotel shows and lounges. Most hotels have happy hours in the early evening. Such places as the Jockey Club, Brannigans, and the Palm Wine Bar are popular with local expatriates. So are Chinese nightclubs, such as the Grand Palace and Golden Million. Many hotels, such as the Neptune, Lido, and Tropicana contain theater restaurants which stage lavish cabaret shows. Singapore's largest disco, the Warehouse, has a dance floor large enough for five hundred people.

Night cruises in the harbor begin at the world trade center ferry building.

Educational Opportunities

College credit programs are available through the ISS International School College Program, the Singapore Institute of Management, and Golden Gate University. The National University of Singapore offers non-credit courses in a variety of subjects. The International Correspondence School on Anson Road offers correspondence courses with career emphases.

There are many opportunities for personal development here. The Nanyang Academy of Fine Arts offers art courses. Mr. Choo Chun teaches Chinese brush painting. Bird watching and wildlife walks are available through the Malayan Nature Society. Bridge and chess clubs abound. It is all here: cooking and crafts, dancing, dogs, and dressmaking, flying and flower arranging, jogging, yoga and stamps.

American Community Activities

The American Association of Singapore is the umbrella organization for all American activities. It sponsors picnics and dances on American holidays and provides a forum for coordination of other American organizations. The American Business Council has monthly meetings which feature speakers on cultural and economic topics. The American Club, located near the Orchard Road shopping district, recently completed construction of a clubhouse containing a coffee shop, dining room, library, lounge, game room, bowling alley, tennis and squash courts, and swimming pool. The club sponsors dinner dances, Sunday brunches, movies, parties, and holiday celebrations. Classes and activities are available for both adults and children. The American Women's Association of Singapore, the most active expatriate women's organization in Singapore, meets the second Tuesday of each month.

Other organizations on the island which are open to Western expatriates include the Economic Society of Singapore which sponsors an annual dinner and symposium, the Masonic Club, Rotary Club, and International Chamber of Commerce. The Singapore Business and Professional Women's Association holds monthly meetings which alternate between evening buffet dinners and afternoon teas. The Singapore Town Club is a social organization which sponsors luncheon meetings for business executives. Some clubs, such as the Singapore Petroleum Club, are related to specific industries. The Petroleum Club's auxiliary, the Oilwives Club, holds a monthly luncheon program the fourth Tuesday of each month. The Oilwives canasta games start at nine A.M. and are so popular reservations are required.

13. Useful Addresses

This chapter lists useful addresses and phone numbers. No attempt has been made to include all addresses. The purpose is to help you get started. Hotels and restaurants listed here are suitable for business.

Accounting and Tax Services

Arthur Andersen & Co.
5 Shenton Way
#31-00 UIC Building
Singapore 0106
Tel: 220-4377

Peat Marwick
16 Raffles Quay
#22-00 Hong Leong Bldg.
Singapore 0104
Tel: 220-7411

Singapore Society of
  Accountants
116 Middle Road
#09-02/04 ICD
Enterprise House
Singapore 0718

Deloitte, Haskins, & Sells
6 Battery Road//27-01
Standard Chartered Bank Bldg.
Singapore 0104
Ph: 224-8288

Price Waterhouse
6 Battery Road
#32-00 Standard
Chartered Bank
Singapore 0104
Tel: 225-6066

Tax Plan Services
1 Scotts Road #15-03
Shaw Center
Singapore 0922

American Organizations in Singapore

The American Association
of Singapore
60 King's Road
Singapore
Tel: 468-6157

American Business Council
354 Orchard Road
#10-12 Shaw House
Singapore
Tel: 235-0077

The American Club
21 Scotts Road
Singapore 0922
Tel: 737-3411

American Women's Association
of Singapore
21 Scott's Road
Singapore 0922
Tel: 737-3411

Banks (American) in Singapore

Bank of America
24 Raffles Place
Clifford Center
Tel: 535-3322

Chase Manhattan Bank
50 Raffles Place
Shell Tower
Tel: 224-2888

Citibank NA
5 Shenton Way
#06-00 UIC Building
Tel: 224-2611

First National Bank of Chicago
76 Shenton Way
#13-00 Ong Building
Tel: 223-9933

Car Rentals in Singapore

Avis
7 Singapore Forum Hotel
Tel: 737-7870

Best Car Rental
Unit 220,
Coronation Shopping
Plaza, Bukit Timah Road
Tel: 489-9777

Blue Star Rental
119 Balestier Road
Tel: 253-4661

Hertz Rent-a-Car
G46-49 World Trade Center
Maritime Square
Tel: 278-1610

Sintat Rent-A-Car
G27 OUB Building
Collyer Quay
Tel: 224-4155

Sunrise Rent-a-Car
107 Bukit Timah Rd.
Tel: 336-0626

Chamber of Commerce

Singapore International Chamber of Commerce
6 Raffles Quay
#06-00 Denmark House
Ph: 224-1255

Dental Services

Singapore Dental Board
Ministry of Health
#09-00 Cuppage Center
55 Cuppage Road

Employment Agencies

The Commissioner of Labor
Ministry of Labor
78 Princep Street
Singapore 0718

Hospitals

American Hospital
321 Joot Chiat Place
Singapore
Tel: 744-7588

Jurong Hospital
241 Corporation Drive
Singapore
Tel: 265-0611

114Doing Business With Singapore

Mount Elizabeth Hospital
3 Mount Elizabeth Road
Singapore
Tel: 737-2666

National University Hospital
5 Lower Kent Ridge Road
Singapore
Tel: 779-5555

Hotels in Singapore

Apollo Singapore
405 Havelock Road
Tel: 733-2081

Century Park
Sheraton Singapore
Nassim Hill
Tel: 732-1222

Dynasty
320 Orchard Road
Tel: 734-9900

Hilton International
Singapore
581 Orchard Road
Tel: 737-2233

Holiday Inn Parkview
11 Cavenaugh Road
Tel: 733-8333

Hyatt Regency Singapore
10-12 Scott's Road
Tel: 733-1288

Mandarin Singapore
333 Orchard Road
Tel: 737-4411

Marina Mandarin
6 Raffles Blvd #01-100
Marina Square
Tel: 338-3388

Ming Court Hotel
1 Tanglin Road
Tel: 737-1133

Orchard Hotel Singapore
442 Orchard Road
Tel: 734-7766

Pavilion Intercontinental
Singapore
1 Cuscaden Road
Tel: 733-8888

Peninsula Hotel
3 Coleman Street
Tel: 337-8091

Plaza Hotel
7500 A Beach Road
Tel: 298-0011

Raffles Hotel
1-2 Beach Road
Tel: 337-8041

Shangri-la Hotel Singapore
22 Orange Grove Road
Tel: 737-3644

Westin Plaza & Westin Stamford
2 Stamford Road
Tel: 733-8585

Housing Agents in Singapore

ERA Realty Network Pte.,
   Ltd.
55 Cuppage Road
#05-05 Cuppage Center
Tel: 732-2866

JC Properties
1 Tanglin Road
#03-258 Podium Block
Ming Court Hotel
Tel: 235-7566

Jones Lang Wooton
65 Chulia Street
#03-05 OCBC Center
Tel: 532-3888

Lindtrac Services Pte., Ltd.
6001 Beach Road
#10-04 Golden Mile Tower
Tel: 294-8879

International Executive Training Programs

Business Training and
   Development Institute
The American University
3301 New Mexico Avenue
   Suite 244
Washington, D.C. 20016

American Graduate School
   of International Business
Thunderbird Campus
Glendale, Arizona 85306

Language Schools

Akizuki Japanese Language
   School
Blk 1, Rochor Road #03-590
Rochor Center, Singapore
Tel: 292-7808

Pacific International
   Language School
1451 South King Street-
   Ste. 404
Honolulu, Hawaii 96814
Ph: (808) 946-8485

116   *Doing Business With Singapore*

Relocation and Orientation Companies

Orientations: Transition Support Services
#5-28 Peninsula Plaza
111 North Bridge Road
Singapore 0617
Tel: 339-0233

Restaurants: Chinese

Ban Seng
79 New Bridge Road
(Teochew Style)

Beng Hiang
20 Murray Street
(Hokkien Style)

Dragon City Restaurant
Novotel Orchin Inn
(Szechuan Style)

Dragon Phoenix Restaurant
Blk 26 Outram Park #06-445
(Variety of Styles)

Eastern Palace
Supreme House
Penang Road
(Peking Style)

Majestic
31 Bukit Pasoh Road
(Cantonese Style)

Moi Kong
25 Murray Street
(Hakka Style)

Omei Restaurant
Hotel Grand Central
(Szechuan Style)

Pine Court Restaurant
Mandarin Hotel
(Peking Style)

Shanghai Palace Restaurant
Excelsior Hotel
(Shanghai Style)

Restaurants: Indian

Annalakshmi
5 Coleman Street
(Vegetarian)

Omar Khayyam
55 Hill Street
(Northern Indian)

Restaurants: Japanese

Hoshogaoka
Apollo Hotel
Nadaman
Shangri-la Hotel

Kobe
Tanglin Shopping Center
Shima
Goodwood Park Hotel

Restaurants: Malay and Indonesian

Aziza's
36 Emerald Hill Road
(Malay)

Bintang Timur
Far East Plaza
(Indonesian)

Kartini
24 Murray Street
(Indonesian)

Satay Club
Queen Elizabeth Walk
(Malay)

Restaurants: Nonya (Straits Chinese-Malay Creole)

Luna Coffee House
Apollo Hotel

Nonya and Baba
262-264 River Valley Road

Restaurants: Other

Go Ryeo Jeong
Orchard Plaza
(Korean)

Her Sea Palace
#01-16 Forum Gallerie
Orchard Road (Thai)

Maxim's de Paris
Pavilion Intercontinental
(French)

Pete's Place
Hyatt Hotel
(Italian)

Saigon Restaurant
#04-03 Cairnhill Place
(Vietnamese)

Stables Grill
Mandarin Hotel
(English)

Schools and Universities in Singapore

Far Eastern Academy
800 Thomson Road
Tel: 253-1155

Golden Gate University
23 Outram Park #03-129
Tel: 220-5877

The International School
Preston Road
Tel: 475-4188

ISS International School
Preston Road
Tel: 475-4188

Singapore American School
60 King's Road
Tel: 466-5611

Singapore Institute of
    Management
15 Scott's Road
#04-13 Thong Teck Bldg.
Tel: 737-8866

Singapore Government Agencies

Customs and Excise
    Controller
Maxwell Road
Singapore 106
Tel: 222-3511

Economic Development
    Board
1 Maritime Square
#10-40 World Trade Center
Singapore 0409

Embassy of Republic of
    Singapore
1824 R Street N.W.
Washington, D.C. 20009
(202) 667-7555/8

Immigration Department
Empress Place
Singapore 0617

Jurong Town Corporation
Jurong Town Hall
301 Jurong Town Hall Road
Singapore 2260

Public Utilities Board
111 Somerset Road
Singapore
Tel: 235-6841

Ministry of Trade and
   Industry
World Trade Center-2nd Fl.
Singapore 0409

Registrar of Businesses
1, Colombo Court #06-06/16
North Bridge Road
Singapore 0617

Registrar of Companies
1, Colombo Court #06-06/16
North Bridge Road
Singapore 0617

Tourist Promotion Board
342 Madison Avenue.
   Ste. 1008
New York, N.Y. 10173
Tel: (212) 687-0385

Tourist Promotion Board
8484 Wilshire Blvd.-Ste.510
Beverly Hills, Calif. 90211
Tel: (213) 852-1901

Tourist Promotion Board
Raffles City Tower #36-04
250 North Bridge Road
Singapore 0617
Tel: 339-6622

Trade Development Board
1 Maritime Square
#03-01 World Trade Center
Singapore 0409

Work Permit Department
80 Prinsep Street
Singapore 0718
Tel: 337-0122

U.S. Government Agencies

Agency for International
   Development
Washington, D.C. 20523

Department of Agriculture
Foreign Agricultural Service
Washington, D.C. 20250

Export-Import Bank of the
   United States
811 Vermont Ave. NW
Washington, D.C. 20571

International Trade
   Administration
Department of Commerce
14th St. & Constitution Ave. NW
Washington, D.C. 20230

Office of the United States
Trade Representative
600 17th Street NW
Washington, D.C. 20501

Overseas Private Investment
    Corporation
1129 20th Street NW
Washington, D.C. 20527

Small Business Administration
Office of International Trade
1441 L Street NW
Washington, D.C. 20416

U.S. Embassy
30 Hill Street
Singapore
Tel: 338-0251

14. Additional Reading

Amin, Mohamed, and Caldwell, Malcolm. *Malaya: the Making of a Neo-Colony*. Nottingham: Spokesman Books, 1977. An interesting series of readings on the economic and political history of Singapore.

Backhouse, Sally. *Singapore*. Harrisburg, Pa.: Stackpole Books, 1973. Excellent rendition of Singapore's history to 1973.

Bendahmane, Unterman. *International Negotiation: Art and Science*. Washington, D.C.: U.S. Government Printing Office, 1984. Report on Conference on International Negotiation, 9-10 June, 1983.

Binnendijk, Hans. *National Negotiating Styles*. Washington D.C.: U.S. Government Printing Office, 1987.

Chambers, Kevin. *The Traveler's Guide to Asian Customs and Manners*. New York: Meadowbrook, 1988.

Cohen, Herb. *You Can Negotiate Anything*. Secaucus, NJ.: Lyle Stuart, 1980.

Collins, Maurice. *Raffles*. New York: The John Day Company, 1966.

Craig, JoAnn. *Culture Shock: Singapore & Malaysia*. Singapore: Times Books International, 1986.

Djamour, Judith. *Malay Kinship and Marriage in Singapore*. New York: Humanities Press. 1965.

Geiger, Theodore. *Tales of Two City-States: The Development Progress of Hong Kong and Singapore*. Washington, D.C.: National Planning Association, 1973.

Gillet, Chris, et.al. (ed.). *Living in Singapore,* Singapore: The American Association of Singapore, 1987.

Guide to Doing Business in Singapore. Singapore: National Printers, Ltd., 1987. The best reference for business regulations, incentives, taxes. Written for Deloitte, Haskins, Sells.

Kuo, Eddie C.Y. and Wong, Ancine, K. (ed.). *The Contemporary Family in Singapore: Structure and Change.* Singapore: Singapore University Press, 1979.

Mahathir bin Mohamad. *The Malay Dilemma.* Singapore: Asian Pacific Press, 1970.

Norman, Henry. *The People and Politics of the Far East.* New York: Charles Scribner's Sons, 1895. One of the best descriptions of Singapore at the end of the nineteenth century.

Nussbaum, Bruce. *The World After Oil: The Shifting Axis of Power and Wealth.* New York: Simon and Schuster, 1983.

Skeat, Walter William. *Malay Magic.* London: MacMillan, 1900. A classic work on Malay animism.

Ronen, Simcha. *Comparative and Multinational Management.* New York: John Wiley and Sons, 1986. An excellent analysis of cultural differences relating to management.

Schumann, Boward. *The International Job Hunting Guide.* New York: John Wiley and Sons, Inc., 1988.

Singapore Official Guide. Singapore: Singapore Promotion Board, 1989. Free upon request.

Warshaw, Steven. *Southeast Asia Emerges.* San Francisco: Canfield Press, 1964.

Welty, Paul Thomas. *The Asians: Their Heritage and Their Destiny,* 5th ed. Philadelphia: J.B. Lippincott and Company, 1976.

Woronoff, Jon. *Asia's "Miracle" Economies.* Seoul: Si-sa-yong-o-sa, Inc., 1986. An excellent study of the relationship of public economic policy to business development in Japan, Taiwan, Korea, Singapore, and Hong Kong.

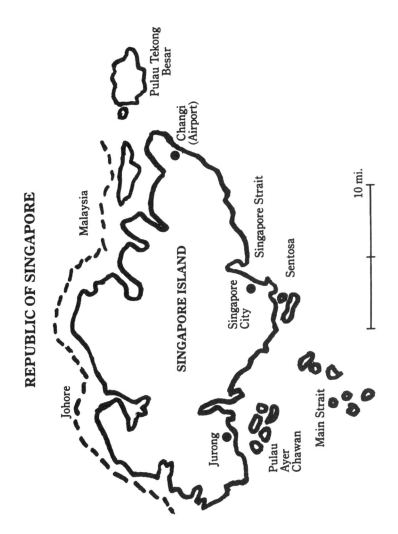

REPUBLIC OF SINGAPORE

Malaysia

Johore

Pulau Tekong
Besar

Changi
(Airport)

SINGAPORE ISLAND

Singapore Strait

Singapore
City

Sentosa

Jurong

Pulau
Ayer
Chawan

Main Strait

10 mi.

INDEX

Global Business Series
from
Jain Publishing Company

Doing Business with Taiwan
ISBN 0-87573-041-8 (paper)
PRICE: $12.95

Doing Business with Korea
ISBN 0-87573-043-4 (paper)
PRICE: $12.95

Doing Business with Singapore
ISBN 0-87573-042-6 (paper)
PRICE: $12.95

Doing Business with Thailand
ISBN 0-87573-044-2 (paper)
PRICE: $12.95

Doing Business with China
ISBN 0-87573-045-0 (paper)
PRICE: $12.95

Doing Business with Mexico
ISBN 0-87573-046-9 (paper)
PRICE: $12.95

ORDER FORM

ORDERED BY:

Name _____

Street _____

_____

City/State/Zip _____

Daytime Phone No. (____) _____

QTY	TITLE	PRICE EACH	TOTAL AMOUNT

POSTAGE & HANDLING		
	Subtotal	
	California residents add 8.25% sales tax	
	Add Postage & Handling	
$3.00 First Book $0.50 Each Add'l.	UPS-Ground add $5.00 additional	
	GRAND TOTAL	

Make check or money order (U.S. dollars) payable to Jain Publishing Company.

MasterCard   VISA

Card No. _____

Exp. Date _____

Signature _____

Ordering by Mail:

Customers using credit cards need only to fold their completed order form in half, tape or staple the free ends and add the correct postage.

Customers paying by check or money order must use an envelope.

Ordering by Phone or Fax:

Credit card customers can order by calling or faxing their filled out order form as follows:

**Jain Publishing Company
Tel (510) 659-8272
Fax (510) 659-0501**

Please allow up to four weeks from receipt of order for delivery. Thank you!

Cut Along Dotted Line

Place
Stamp
Here

**Jain Publishing Company
P.O. Box 3523
Fremont, CA 94539**

Attn: Order Department